D0712144

Southeast Asian Exodus:
From Tradition to Resettlement

Understanding Refugees from
Laos, Kampuchea and Vietnam in Canada

Elliot L. Tepper, Editor

A Publication by The Canadian Asian Studies Association

Canadian Cataloguing in Publication Data
Main entry under title:

Southeast Asian exodus

Issued also in French under title: *D'un continent à un autre.*
  Bibliography: p.
  ISBN 0-920296-08-4

  1. Asia, Southeastern — Civilization. 2. Refugees — Asia, Southeastern.
  3. Refugees — Canada. I. Tepper, Elliot L. II. Canadian Asian Studies
  Association.

  DS532.8.S68   959   C80-090092-8

First Printing, 1980   10 9 8 7 6 5 4 3 2

Published in Canada in 1980
by The Canadian Asian Studies Association
3A61 Paterson Hall, Carleton University, Ottawa, K1S 5B6

Cover: *Children in a Vietnamese Refugee Camp, Songkhla, Thailand.* Photo by
Ian Hamilton

Section pages: Drawings are traditional symbols of Vietnam, Laos and
Cambodia. Illustrations by Lily Chi.

Cover Design by Margaret Finnegan

Typesetting by Professional Graphics

Contents

French Protectorate and the Independence Period; the
Cambodian Refugees.
The Traditional Khmer Way of Life
Crops; Livestock; Fish; Transportation; Land Tenure;
Industry; Diet; Dress; the House; the Cities; Cambodian
Society; Family Organization.
Religious Structure
Theravada Buddhism; Islàm in Cambodia; Mahayana
Buddhism; Christianity; the New Year (Cul Chnam Tigey); the
Sacred Furrow; the Triple Anniversary of Buddha.
The Cambodia of Tomorrow

Family, Wat, and Village
The House; "Come and Take Rice"; Buddhism — the Gentle
Way; Bouns (Festivals) and the Baci.
"Many Girls' Names are Flowers" (a Modern Lao Legend)
A Note on Pronunciation

History of Chinese Influence in Southeast Asia
The Economic and Political Power of the Chinese in Southeast
Asia
Structure of Chinese Communities
The Policy of the Chinese Government
Vietnam's Ethnic Chinese Refugees
Kampuchea's Ethnic Chinese Refugees

The Corner of Asia
The Environment
The Agriculture
External Influences

Characteristics of the Continental Realm
The Case of Indochina; the Distribution of Population in East
Indochina; Importance of Agriculture.

Acknowledgements

One measure of the response to the refugee crisis is the co-operation that was given in preparing this complex venture. As editor, my first thanks must go to the contributors who broke all rules of academic publishing by writing and editing quickly, clearly, and cordially. Additional assistance was provided by our Refugee Committee.

Government agencies, too, have provided unusual moral and financial support at key stages in the evolution of this volume. Publication was made possible by the generous funding assistance of the Multiculturalism Program, Government of Canada, which we acknowledge with appreciation and thanks. Beyond this, Dr. Richard K. Young, of the Multiculturalism Directorate of the Secretary of State has been a good friend who rendered invaluable assistance.

Similarly, the Refugee Task Force and Indo-Chinese Refugee Settlement Grant Program of Employment and Immigration Canada, have supplied information and financial support to permit the Canadian Asian Studies Association to proceed with refugee-related projects. Kirk Bell and Michael Molloy were specially helpful in this regard.

Provincially, we have received encouragement from the Ontario Ministry of Culture and Recreation, in particular Estelle Reed in Toronto and Gail Silverberg in Ottawa.

Special thanks must go as well to Sharon Russo and Alan Clarke of Project 4000 in Ottawa. They provided a forum from which we all benefited, by presenting early versions of these chapters to an audience of sponsor groups and others directly involved with Asian refugees.

Translation from French to English, chapters two and five, was by Sinclair Robinson. Translation from English to French, chapters one, three, four, six, seven, nine, ten, acknowledgements, introduction, and conclusion, was by Jean Miquet; and chapters eight, eleven, twelve, and thirteen by Louis Kovacs.

Elliot L. Tepper
Ottawa, July, 1980

Introduction

The Need to Know

The Need To Know

by
Elliot L. Tepper

Knowledge about Indochina is limited, and the need for it is suddenly great. Even without the refugee crisis, this cockpit of war would be of great interest. Victory for the revolutionary forces led to a new era for the region, but not peace. The time is ripe for a fresh interpretation of an area so long obscured by emotions and conflict. The refugee crisis adds urgency to the need for information as people of many states and from many segments of the host communities meet people from Indochina, frequently for the first time. For all concerned, the result could be mutually enriching or socially traumatic. The Asian diaspora has been welcomed; now it must be understood.

The Canadian Experience

Refugees are history's orphans. They are one dimension of the ideological and political conflicts that beset our world. Revolutions and war are the hallmarks of our age, and refugees the grim by-products. Refugees are not immigrants, people who voluntarily depart their homelands to seek a better life. They are emergencies: the homeless, the stateless, the dispossessed.

Communities may be judged by treatment accorded orphans, and the world community is not an exception. Treatment of refugees has varied from shameful to inspirational, from hypocritical to heroic. No generalization can adequately encompass the response to all refugees, over time, everywhere. However, Canadian response to Indochinese refugees can be put into perspective. Whatever the past record — in regard to Sikhs aboard the ship *Komagata Maru*, European Jewry seeking asylum from Hitler, or Canadian Japanese citizens at the time of Pearl Harbor — Canada has responded to crisis in Southeast Asia with an unprecedented program of large-scale admission and resettlement. The 60,000 so far permitted by government guidelines constitute a larger number than recent equivalent programs for Hungarian, Ugandan Asian, or Chilean refugees.

As interesting as the total number involved is the shared responsibility of government and private sponsorship. This is an immediate, positive, and long-lasting benefit of the Canadian response. In the future, the refugees will contribute in material and cultural ways to Canada's mosaic. They will add numbers to a country approaching a negative growth rate in population; they will supply willing labour in markets Canadians no longer readily fill; they will infuse entrepreneurial talent into a sluggish economy; and they will bring cultural richness and diversity to a multicultural society. But the most tangible benefit to Canada is the joining together of neighbour with neighbour, of citizen with government, even prior to the arrival of the refugees. At a time when the basic fabric of Canada was being questioned, the answer came that the national spirit was one of co-operation, sacrifice, and humanitarian generosity.

Estimates provided by the government's Refugee Task Force and elsewhere indicate the depth of general involvement. Canada is a world leader, on a per capita basis, in the admission of Indochinese refugees; for the size of the country's population, the 60,000 admissions so far pledged place Canada in the first rank of accepting countries. Private sponsorship exceeded all expectations, reducing direct government sponsorship well below the 50 percent matching basis originally indicated at the outset of the crisis. Indeed, private sector response has been so great that government policy remains under pressure to lift the present ceiling and permit additional refugees to enter. At a minimum, based on cautious use of figures, at least 65,000 individuals are directly and immediately involved in sponsorship activity. A substantially wider circle of people is involved, through financial donations, in supporting officially registered sponsor groups. Beyond that are people who volunteer time to sponsorship activities, from large umbrella networks, such as Operation Lifeline in southern Ontario, to the Saturday evening benefit dances at local community centres across Canada. The total number of people touched by the refugee experience, and the effect upon them, is incalculable.

Moreover, the effect is just beginning. The transition from refugee to new Canadian will involve neighbours, teachers, employers. No doubt, it will also involve social workers, doctors, community resource persons, and a wide range of government officials. The sponsorship program, in both its private and government components, sees to it that the settlement process will occur throughout the country, in small towns as well as major cities. There may be secondary migration as refugees move from their places of original arrival to cities large enough to give them the ethnic, cultural, and economic opportunity that has always drawn people to a metropolis. But the nature of the sponsorship program insures that this group of refugees will remain widely dispersed for a long period and enter deeply into the social fabric.

Format of the Book

The book is divided into three parts, with all the chapters designed to assist the reader in understanding the refugee crisis and its aftermath. Part one contains chapters on the countries and peoples of Indochina. Taken together, the section presents an interpretation of the history and culture of Indochina. Part two offers overviews of the human geography and recent political history of the area as a whole and examines the regional impact of the refugee crisis. Part three consists of chapters relating to specific aspects of the resettlement process. A brief conclusion speculates about the future. Thus, information and interpretation follow the path of the refugee from rich historical tradition, through crisis, to problems and promise of a new life in a new homeland.

Part One PEOPLES AND CULTURES

Indochina is where the cultural spheres of India and China meet. The resulting amalgam has produced distinct civilizations and traditions. Authors in this section present a view of these distinct cultures, country by country. Since half or more of the refugees coming to Canada from Indochina are ethnically Chinese, a separate background chapter has been provided.

Appropriately, the opening chapter is on Vietnam, the focus of turmoil for more than thirty years. Professor N.H. Chi provides an important reinterpretation of Vietnamese history, giving a cultural interpretation that explains nationalism, village life and attitudes towards neighbouring states and many other things, all as part of his illumination of the refugee situation. Perspective on the crisis is what all authors were asked to provide. Professor Chi is well suited to do so. He is a political scientist, originally from Vietnam, who has long been active in refugee resettlement activities in North America.

Cambodia is given unusual attention in this volume, more than is typically the case. Specific detail is given in three separate contributions, and general commentaries appear in many other chapters as well. We have attempted to compensate for the usual neglect of this country because of the dimensions of its refugee situation. One of the great civilizations of Asia may be nearing extinction. There is an understandable urge to explain the fact and to preserve what knowledge we have of its past. For that reason, it is especially fortunate that Robert Garry has written a substantial chapter on the country he knows as few other scholars know it. Long a professor of geography at the University of Montreal and now retired, he spent fifteen years of his early career in Cambodia.

Laos also is frequently mentioned by our authors. Although it provides the fewest refugees to the Asian exodus and is less often in the news, it is a country known for its graceful and charming cultural characteristics. It is perhaps appropriate that our Lao specialist has chosen to interpret the country through a Lao parable and to present its cultural attributes almost as a poem. Peter Royle lived in a Lao village environment and was considered "family" before, during, and after the revolution. He taught English there and in Sabah, and his chapter was written from Ungava, Quebec, where at present he teaches Inuit (Eskimo) children while completing his thesis on Laos for Carleton University.

Overseas Chinese, the "alien sojourners," have been prominent in the refugee overflow from the region. The chapter provided here gives detail on the position of the Chinese community in each of the countries of the region, a general account of overseas Chinese, and one of several interpretations in the book of the causes of conflict and refugee departure. Professor Willmott is one of the world's leading authorities on overseas Chinese and one of the only scholars on the Chinese in Cambodia. After teaching in Canada for many years, he now makes his home in New Zealand.

Part Two   LANDS AND POLITICS

This section opens with two chapters that view the region as a whole and explore the factors that give it both unity and diversity. Professor De Koninck explains the origin and movements of the people of the region and their ecology, the relationship of man to environment. Professor Wurfel provides an interpretation of the political interactions that over time have shaped the history of the region and led ultimately to the refugee crisis. Together these two chapters provide frameworks that give the reader a perspective on the past, present, and future of the Indochinese people. Professor De Koninck, who teaches geography at Laval University, is a prolific author who makes frequent trips to Southeast Asia. Professor Wurfel teaches political science at the University of Windsor. A widely respected authority, he is a mainstay of Asian studies in Canada, both academically and organizationally.

Asia's refugees are not Asia's problem only but a problem for the world community. Richard Stubbs shows the hardship, political and economic, that the refugee influx placed upon the states of first refuge in Asia. No state in Asia is without domestic tension, which new refugees exacerbate. He answers the question, Why can't they stay in Southeast Asia? Suteera Thomson studies the Thai situation specifically. Thailand is a major recipient of refugees and the largest repository of Khmer nationals. She explains the complexity of the Thai response and provides detail about an important Canadian initiative to find ways to keep the Khmer people near their homeland. Richard Stubbs teaches political science at St. Francis Xavier University and is a specialist on Southeast Asian politics. Suteera Thomson, science adviser to the Science Council of Canada, is originally from Thailand and recently spent two months completing arrangements for the establishment of a refugee camp to be run by the Canadian University Service Overseas (CUSO).

Part Three PROBLEMS OF RESETTLEMENT

All our authors are aware of both the necessity and hazards of generalizations. No statement can hold true for 60,000 individuals, yet as Asian specialists we can provide some insights that might prove essential in the period of adaptation. To compound our unease, generalizations about resettlement in North America must be based on slender evidence as the experience so far is recent and little documented; yet to say nothing would be a disservice to those who have a great and immediate need to know. Therefore, the authors of section three have willingly braved the hazards.

Canadian immigration policy is both explained and critically explored by the authors of chapter nine. The chapter examines the Canadian case, providing a well-rounded picture and base for comparison. Howard Adelman is a professor of philosophy at

York University and chief animateur of Operation Lifeline, the country's largest umbrella sponsorship organization. Charles Le Blanc is a sinologist at the University of Montreal who took an early interest in encouraging research on Asian refugees in Canada. Jean-Philippe Thérien is his energetic research assistant and co-author.

The next three chapters are by professionals who have applied their training to assisting refugee resettlement. Between them they explore some of the most sensitive areas of the entire resettlement process. All do so knowing the benefits and pitfalls of generalization. Their findings are based on field research in Asia and North America as well as extensive personal involvement with refugee activity. Food, kinship, cultural habits, ethnic rivalry, economic adaptation, and many other topics are covered in these far-ranging chapters. Penny Van Esterik is a specialist in Southeast Asian cultural anthropology who has recently moved to Cornell University from Notre Dame University. Doreen Indra and Norman Buchignani are in the Departments of Sociology and Anthropology respectively at the University of Alberta, Edmonton.

The resettlement process has recognizable stages for both successful and troubled new arrivals. Recognition of normal and disturbed reactions may be essential for those involved in assisting cultural adjustment. Dr. Matthew Suh has presented clear, useful advice, based on his medical training and experience with refugees. Originally from Asia, Dr. Suh is director of adult psychiatry at the Royal Ottawa Hospital and associate professor of psychiatry at the University of Ottawa.

David Wurfel's concluding comments focus on human rights. He offers some policy suggestions to governments concerned with assisting refugees and bringing peace to the region.

Conclusion: Southeast Asian Exodus and the Canadian Asian Studies Association

Controversy is a likely product of this book. There is no official history or established consensus about people and events in Asia or the nature of the resettlement process. Our authors disagree with each other on some points and express themselves in different ways. No attempt has been made to force agreement or impose a uniform style of expression. Even some overlap of material has been permitted to maintain the integrity and useful-ness of individual contributions. The contributors have been asked to take part in this volume because of their scholarship and their willingness to help further understanding.

The Canadian Asian Studies Association is pleased to provide this book to the general public and to our students, present and future. Because of the need for information, the authors all worked under intense pressure and in haste. We would all wish for more time to present our ideas and additional material. However, the refugee crisis will not go away, and the settlement process will only evolve into further stages. The association welcomes comments on this publication and looks forward to providing additional publications if the need to know remains.

Part One

Peoples and Cultures

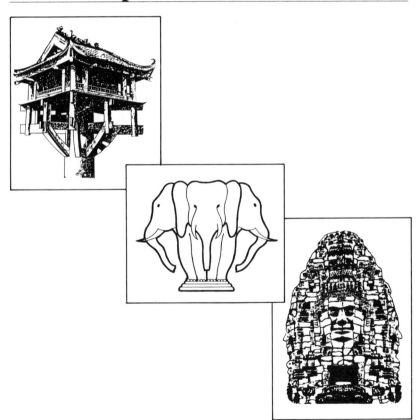

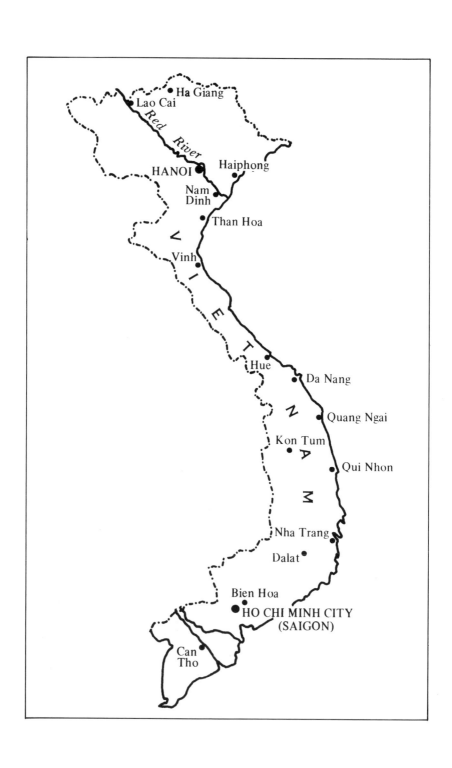

1

Vietnam:

The Culture of War

by
N.H. Chi

Territorial Imperatives

Vietnam — "the pearl of the Orient," the "Southeast Asian balcony on the Pacific" — is one of the three Indochinese states that have been in the headlines of major newspapers for the last three decades. In contrast to its military reputation against world powers — France, the United States, and China — Vietnam is a relatively small country with a population of more than 50 million inhabitants and an area one-third the size of British Columbia. Yet, the territorial factor has always played a dominant role in the ancient and modern history of Vietnam and of the Indochinese peninsula.

The Dawn of History and the Peasant-Soldiers

The early history of Vietnam is derived more from legends and myths than from facts. The Vietnamese believe that their country has four thousand years of civilization.

Vietnam was originally known as Van-Lang and was founded by Hung-Vuong I in the Red River delta (North Vietnam). The first dynasty was called Hong-Bang (2879 - 258 B.C.?), probably derived from the name of the river Hong-Ha (Red River) whose annual floods have fertilized the rice fields with its rich, reddish alluvium.

Unlike numerous nomadic tribes living in the mountainous regions, the delta people started to develop a strong cultural

identity based on rice cultivation and fishing, and constantly reinforced by legends about their origin and their struggles for their
cultural survival. According to one of the legends passed on from
one generation to the next, the Vietnamese people are descendants
of Au-Co (a fairy) and Lac-Long-Quan (the Dragon Spirit). This
legend and numerous others told to the children up to the present
time have undoubtedly strengthened the Vietnamese cultural
identity and national pride. At least, this helped the Vietnamese
in countering the process of Sinification during the next one
thousand years of Chinese domination, from 111 B.C. to 939 A.D.

Under the Chinese rule, the Vietnamese readily absorbed
modern agricultural techniques such as rice cultivation, irrigation, and flood control as well as socio-political structures imported
from the north, including Confucian education, the mandarin
system, postal services, and national currency. While upper class
Vietnamese were co-opted into the colonial system, the peasants
remained untouched by the Sinification process. On the contrary,
they had to carry the burden of modernization in the form of heavy
taxes and forced labour. Peasant uprisings against the colonial
government were not uncommon, especially when they were led
by individuals from Chinese-educated families such as Lady
Trieu-Au (248 B.C.), the Trung sisters (39 A.D.), or Lord Li-Bon
(542 A.D.).

Throughout ten centuries of Chinese rule, and numerous
peasant rebellions, an historical pattern has arisen that has
persisted to the present time.

1. In the minds of the Vietnamese people, the northern threat
    against their national survival has always been a real and
    crucial factor that no Vietnamese leader can afford to neglect.
2. During their painful confrontation with China — and later
    with the West — the Vietnamese have shown their exceptional
    ability to learn and to adapt while maintaining their cultural
    identity, especially at the village level.
3. Peasant dissatisfaction has always been the key to any
    successful campaign against foreign domination. For
    example, the twenty-three-year-old Trieu-Au had a tragic
    end because she failed to mobilize the rural masses to her
    side. In contrast, the Trung sisters and Li-Bon had led the
    peasants to victories because they fully realized that they
    could never have succeeded in defeating China without rural
    support. It may be said that the Trung sisters were the first

Vietnamese leaders who successfully used the "people's war" strategy against their foreign enemy. Unfortunately, Queens Trung-Trac and Trung-Nhi — like Emperor Li-Bon five centuries later — could not maintain the independence of Vietnam for more than a few years. China was too strong, and the Vietnamese society was still too disorganized, with its archaic social-political structures, to be able to resist the Chinese expeditionary forces. In other words, Vietnam was not modernized (that is, Sinified) enough to be able to challenge its northern neighbour. At any rate, these short periods of independence did keep the national spirit alive in the minds of the Vietnamese people.

4.   Each uprising against foreign domination or each war against foreign invasion has had the effect of reinstating the foreign-educated élites with the rural masses. Such an encounter in the battlefield has helped the élites to rediscover their roots and to have a better appreciation of the peasants' miseries and contribution to the nation-building process. On the other hand, modern ideas learned from foreign invaders have had a chance to be transferred from the élites to the rural masses. In short, Vietnamese society has been built and modernized through its numerous wars against foreign invaders. This national development pattern has persisted throughout the history of Vietnam up to the present time.

Independence and Territorial Expansion

At the beginning of the tenth century, China was in a period of internal divisions and decline. Popular uprisings in Vietnam then had a better chance of success. The Vietnamese guerrilla leader Ngo-Quyen, with the support of peasants and fishermen of the Red River, succeeded in overthrowing the colonial regime and defeating two expeditionary forces from the north — the Dienbienphu of the tenth century. China, divided and exhausted, finally had to leave Vietnam alone, at least for the time being.

With independence, the Vietnamese peasants, who had bravely fought and suffered for centuries, had to go through another sixty years of wars between feudal lords before internal peace was established. By the eleventh century, for the first time a central and stable government was set up in Hanoi after all feudal chiefs had been defeated. The society was now transformed into a modern nation-state ready to start its "historical mission" of southward expansion.

Peace was always short in Vietnam. While important public works (construction of canals, dykes, roads, postal services), land claims, social reforms, and other changes were carried out, Vietnam had to be constantly on guard against the threat of invasion and absorption from the north and to be ready for territorial expansion in the south. For centuries, children have been taught to praise those emperors who dedicated themselves to the policy of national reconstruction, economic development, national defence, and territorial expansion.

To carry out this program, an original system of military services was established during the early years of the eleventh century: every year, able young men were to spend six months in the army and six months on their farms; furthermore, if not fighting, soldiers had to work on land development projects such as clearing jungles, building dykes and canals, and draining swamps. Thus, the concept *peasant-soldier* was invented during the early years of the eleventh century as an emergency measure for national survival. The same policy has been adopted by the present regime.

China did not give up her dream of reconquering Vietnam. For example, after building an empire from the Mediterranean to the Pacific, Genghis Khan decided to move to Southeast Asia through Vietnam. In 1284, his grandson sent a huge expeditionary force to remove the Vietnamese obstacle to Southeast Asia. All Vietnamese peasants were mobilized to mount an apparently hopeless resistance. As it turned out, 500,000 Mongols were annihilated in the Red River delta by 200,000 peasant soldiers. The Mongols came back three years later only to be routed again. After this battle, the Mongolian emperor decided to give up, since the cost of conquering Vietnam was too high for its worth. The military history of Vietnam seems to have repeated itself in the twentieth century.

Besides the Chinese threat from the north, Vietnam had to face two powerful countries in the south: Champa and Cambodia. As expected, these two Southeast Asian powers, sometimes with military support from Burma and Thailand, could not match the peasant-soldier war-machine of Vietnam. In fact, as soon as Vietnam became independent and the threat from the north was reduced, the Vietnamese started their territorial expansion into the south. Vietnamese kings used all possible means — either by military campaigns or diplomatic manoeuvres — to extend their land at the expense of their southern neighbours. From one generation to the next, the Cham empire was gradually absorbed into Vietnam. By the end of the sixteenth century, Champa was reduced to a dead civilization. The Khmer empire became the next victim. By the end of the eighteenth century, half of the empire had been absorbed into Vietnam. The arrival of Western powers in Indochina in the nineteenth century put an end to Vietnam's expansionist policy. As a result, the Khmer civilization was saved (maybe temporarily) from extinction to become the modern Kampuchea with Vietnamese advisers and soliders on its soil.

The Vietnamese peasant-soldier system of colonialization was extremely effective and ruthless. Once a district or a province was wrestled from the Champa or Khmer empire, lands were expropriated from the natives and distributed to the peasant-soldiers for cultivation. Thus, as soon as the captured area had been adequately pacified, soldiers' families and landless peasants moved in from the north to cultivate the land and to defend it from its former owners' attacks. In this way, within a very short time after the military victory, a new settlement was established in the form of a village deeply rooted in the new land but still strongly integrated into the old culture. Although Vietnamese historians have said very little about the life of the natives under their new rulers, it is not unreasonable to presume that the Vietnamese method of settlement must have been very brutal to the conquered. Most of the natives were probably killed or forced to leave their homeland to give room to the new settlers, who had neither political nor economic nor military reasons to protect the "human rights" of the natives. At any rate, at the present time the descendants of the once-powerful and highly civilized Champa empire consist of less than 100,000 souls living their miserable lives on the barren hills of Phan-Rang and Phan-Thiet. The ancestors of some 400,000 Cambodians still living along the border of Vietnam and Kampuchea doubtless shared the same fate as the citizens of the Champa empire.

From the reports of the refugees, it seems that the present regime has applied the same method towards the people of South Vietnam: landless peasants have been transferred from the North to cultivate the best lands in the Mekong Delta. Saigon people and other "traitors" are sent to the jungles — the so-called new economic region.

Internal Division: The Weakness of Vietnam

The "March to the South," or Nam-Tien, even though extremely successful in terms of territorial expansion, became a political liability for the leaders of Hanoi in the long run. As the country expanded, it became more and more difficult for the mandarins of Hanoi to maintain effective control over the victorious generals of the south. On the one hand, distance and mountains constituted formidable barriers for the central government to communicate with, and hence communicate with its troops in the south. On the other hand, the method of peasant-soldier settlement, even though effective in the sense of conquering new lands while maintaining cultural links with the northern homeland, very soon become a liability in the sense of national integration. As the territorial expansion proceeded farther into the south, local commanders depended less and less on Hanoi for human and financial resources to support their historical mission of liquidating the Champa and the Khmer empires. Near the end of the sixteenth century, the South became an autonomous region under the nominal leadership of the powerless king of Hanoi.

While fighting for territorial expansion in the South continued, war broke out between North Vietnam and South Vietnam in the name of the kings and national reunification. This fratricidal conflict continued on and off for 150 years. Finally, a peasant uprising in the South under the leadership of a military genius, Nguyen Hue, wiped out both southern and northern regimes. In 1786, Vietnam was at last reunified.

As before, a final victory did not mean peace for the peasants. Two years later, they were called back to defend their nation again. Imperial China's last attempt to conquer Vietnam was quickly crushed by the peasant-soldiers in the famous Tet Offensive of 1788. By this time, the northern threat became utterly irrelevant in comparison with the power and imperialistic ambitions of Western powers.

Western Penetration

Located at the crossroad of the spice route between India and China, Vietnam could not be left alone by Western powers. The Bay of Da-Nang under the control of the southern regime became an outpost for Portuguese traders as early as 1535. Very soon, the Portuguese became the main weapon suppliers for the South, with the hope that a reunified Vietnam under a friendly government would be a good business investment in the long run.

To protect their interests against their trade rivals, Dutch traders adopted the same policy and jumped in to help North Vietnam with their weapons. Thanks to those programs of military assistance in exchange for local currency and for complete freedom to exploit local spice growers, commanders of the North and the South could now inflict heavy casualties on each other's troops, at least at a level unheard of before in the history of Vietnam. Such a policy, relying on foreign assistance to kill one's own people, easily explains the general dissatisfaction of the peasants whose successful uprising under Nguyen Hue brought about national reunification.

Fortunately, Western traders found that they had overestimated their profit margins in their trade with Vietnam. Their military and commercial relationships with Vietnam gradually decreased and were quickly replaced by French Catholic missions. However, soul saving was not the only interest of France in Vietnam. It is not a coincidence that the French East India Company was created in the same year (1664) as the French Society of Foreign Missions. The company was to give financial support to the Catholic missionaries, whereas the latter were to act as the agents of the company. As the head of the Catholic missions in Vietnam reported to the directors of the company in 1667, there were "as many promoters of the Company's progress as there will be bishops, priests, and believers."

The co-operation between the church and the company somewhat irritated Vietnamese officials but did not antagonize them enough to put the Christians in danger. Unfortunately, besides exhorting the Vietnamese to give up their cult of ancestors, the French Catholic missionaries had a tendency to get involved in local politics, especially with rebellion movements. In fact, a number of missionaries were caught among the rebels and sentenced to death. French gunboats were sent to Vietnam to punish the "insolent barbarians." Thus, in the name of God, the French conquest of Indochina started in 1858.

The kings of Cambodia and Laos quickly put their kingdoms under the French protectorate, partly because they knew they could not resist the French colonial ambition, and partly because they did not want to be gradually absorbed into the Vietnamese empire. The independence of Vietnam was terminated by the

Treaty of Protectorate in 1883. However, it took the French colonial government two more decades of intensive military campaigns before it could "pacify" the colony.

After bloody pacification campaigns, which lasted until the beginning of this century, the colonial government started to build up the infrastructures for economic exploitation of the colony. Through a policy of co-option, the former mandarin class became the administrative tool of the new regime. Only a very small number of traditionalist scholars resisted the tempting offers made by the new ruler. Very soon they became relics of the past. As French colonialism became more entrenched on Vietnamese soil, there was indeed no room for alienated poets like Nguyen Du or Tan-Da. Others, like Phan-Boi-Chau and Cuong-De, looking towards China and Japan for help and inspiration, were to be disappointed and expelled from these countries under the pressure of France. The legitimacy of the traditional élite received a deadly blow when Bao-Dai, raised and educated in France, was brought home to become the new emperor of the puppet regime.

When the Vietnamese turned towards the emerging Westernized élite for leadership and guidance, their nationalist aspirations were again frustrated. Most of the French-educated youths were more than happy to replace their Confucian elders in the colonial administration. They became members of a privileged class, economically and culturally segregated from the mass of peasants. Others, with literary inclinations, assigned themselves the task of translating French authors such as La Fontaine or Molière into Vietnamese. Works of "revolutionary" writers like Voltaire or Rousseau were not imported into the colony. Young urban Vietnamese kept themselves busy either participating in the trans-Indochinese bicycle race or crying for their lost loves in the tradition of Lamartine or Chateaubriand. Victor Hugo was introduced into the Vietnamese society and became one of the gods venerated by the Mekong peasants in the Cao-Dai temple.

In general, the gap between the French-educated urban Vietnamese and the mass of peasants was unbridgeable indeed. To be fair, not all Westernized intellectuals were totally dedicated to serving the colonial interests. In fact, traditional national aspirations that were deeply rooted in the Vietnamese culture were now taken up by a number of young intellectuals in the cities. Some of them tried to copy Sun Yat Sen's Chinese nationalist party. Unfortunately, their sentimentalism and their isolation from the rural mass made them unable to cope effectively with the French secret police or the Foreign Legion. After a few years of operation, the entire leadership of the Vietnamese Nationalist party was captured and guillotined. From that day on, this anti-Communist party became a ghost party without any real political power in its confrontation with its rival, the Communist party of Ho Chi Minh.

Thus, by the late 1930s the colonial administration, with its policy of brutal harassment and co-option, managed to undermine the legitimacy of the emerging élite that lived on urban islands in the middle of an ocean of rural miseries. The peasant mass remained in its solitude of backwardness behind the bamboo hedges of its villages, while the new élite lived in the cities and enjoyed the grandeur of the French culture. In this manner, the colony was pacified and Westernized, and Vietnam became the showcase of the French *mission civilisatrice*. As in the case of China, with its Sinification policy twenty centuries ago, France's mission civilisatrice prepared Vietnam for the war of liberation and social revolution.

The colonial system proved quite precarious. Peasants were ruthlessly exploited by absentee landlords whose relationships with their tenants were now motivated by the free-enterprise principle of maximum profit rather than the previous system of traditional paternalism. Rice was to be extracted from the countryside at the maximum yield for exportation in order to finance conspicuous consumption in the cities. Furthermore, expensive programs of public works and subsidies granted to French companies and plantations were based on regressive taxes, such as the head tax and the salt tax imposed on every peasant no matter how poor he was. In addition, the government set up a nation-wide system of distribution of alcoholic beverages and opium as an additional source of revenue for the colonial administration. The countryside was ready for a revolution.

Rural uprisings became more and more frequent in the 1930s and 1940s. Even Chiang Kai-shek and Roosevelt had to admit that "France has had the country . . . for nearly one hundred years, and the people are worse off than at the beginning. . ."

The Communist party under the brilliant leadership of Ho Chi Minh was built up in the countryside under these conditions. His explicit reliance on the rural mass proved to be a stroke of genius in the long run. In fact, when the colonial regime collapsed during the Second World War, Ho Chi Minh with his mass party was the only leader ready to go to the cities to take over the bureaucracy left by the French. Unfortunately, with the help of the British and the Kuomintang Chinese (who were stationed in Indochina to disarm the defeated Japanese), the French Foreign Legion returned. Ho Chi Minh was forced to move his French-created bureaucracy and the urban élite to the country-side for the preparation of a protracted war of resistance.

The movement of French-educated élites to the countryside was an historic encounter between the two alien cultures and it was a shocking experience for both. However, after a short while, the peasants and the Westernized urbanites came to terms, learning from and growing to appreciate each other. All the difficulties and the misunderstanding were dampened in the highly emotional atmosphere of nationalism at this time of crisis. The peasants shared their huts and meagre meals with the well-educated urbanites. The urbanites introduced modern ideas to the peasants. Within two years (1945-46), the illiteracy rate dropped dramatically. Modern administrative structures were set up. New methods of production were tried. Peasants not only learned how to read and write, they also learned about modern thought and relating their daily miseries to global problems. As a result, a new élite was born during the second half of the 1940s from this process of ruralization of French-educated intellectuals.

In summary, ruralization of the Western urbanites created their political legitimacy in the eyes of the peasants, and the urbanization of the countryside engendered revolutionary expectations for the peasants. This was the strength of the Vietnamese guerrillas in both Indochinese wars.

Not surprisingly, a number of bureaucrats and urban intellectuals could not adjust to the rural conditions. They remained foreigners among their own people. Sooner or later, they left and went back to the cities to join their French masters. The old buraucracy was re-created minus the most dedicated and dynamic elements, who preferred to stay in the countryside fighting for their country with the peasants. Thus, the French and their mercenary collaborators were much more isolated from the rural masses than before. Furthermore, the urbanized peasants, now better organized and better led, wanted to capture the cities to fulfil their revolutionary expectations. The French lost their war at the start.

The battle of Dienbienphu (1954) terminated French colonialism in Vietnam. Vietnam was divided again. The French colonial heritage was moved to the South in 1954 and transferred to the American-supported regime of Ngo Dinh Diem. The second Indochinese war had been lost before it started. With Soviet and Chinese weapons, the Vietnamese peasant-soldiers were more than ready to face the American challenge against their desire for national reunification and social revolution.

Cultural Identity

One of the most striking features of the Vietnamese society is the homogeneity of its culture throughout the whole country, in spite of 150 years of partition between North and South Vietnam. The same language, customs, and social structures have prevailed in every Vietnamese village. This cultural characteristic becomes more remarkable when one notices cultural and linguistic diversities among the hundreds of ethnic minority groups that constitute less than 10 percent of the population of Vietnam.

In appearance, the Vietnamese culture (before the birth of the "socialist man" in the near future, as expected by the current government) is very similar to that of China in general and South China in particular. This similarity is undoubtedly the result of a thousand years of Sinification during the early history of Vietnam. The Vietnamese culture is closer to its northern neighbour's than that of Laos and Kampuchea. Yet, anti-Chinese nationalist feeling has been almost an obsession among Vietnamese people in spite of the fact that basic social structures and religious beliefs are practically the same in the two countries. It is obvious that appearances are always misleading, especially when one deals with Vietnam.

In spite of cultural homogeneity throughout Vietnam, both past and present histories show that cultural homogeneity does not necessarily mean political unity. In fact, secession wars, and even territorial partition, were not uncommon among the Vietnamese. These apparent paradoxes are explained by analyzing various social-cultural structures of the Vietnamese society.

Religion

Confucianism, Taoism, and Buddhism were the first three religio-ethical systems introduced in Vietnam and integrated to the native spiritualism already in existence before the arrival of the Chinese. Christianity, or more specifically Roman Catholicism, was imported from the West only very recently.

It is interesting to note that in peacetime, Buddhism tends to be practised mainly by women or retired scholars. Frequently, in times of crisis, Buddhism and Taoism can easily become a politico-religious movement against the central government. For example, Hao-Hoa as a reform Buddhist sect has been, until recently, a political force rallying dissatisfied peasants, first against the French, then against both the Communists of Hanoi and the anti-Communists of Saigon. Similarly, the Cao-Dai temples, where Jesus Christ, Buddha, Confucius, and the French writer Victor Hugo were venerated, have been political centres of peasant rebellion.

At the political level, religions have been used effectively in the past to maintain national identity and national integration. National heroes are venerated in thousands of temples all over the country. Both peasants and village notables go to those temples to pray for miracles and protection against the forces of nature. Parents usually take their children to the local temples, where stories of national victories against Chinese invaders are told with awe and veneration. In general, national hero worship is a synthesis between Confucianism and Taoism mobilized in the service of the Vietnam nation. It is obvious that when the Chinese taught the Vietnamese these religions, they did not expect their Sinification works would be used to maintain and reinforce the Vietnamese identity.

It should be pointed out that the Vietnamese, unlike traditional Japanese, do not treat their superiors as being of sacred origin. Only Hung-Vuong I is annually venerated, not because he was the emperor representing the soul of Vietnam, but because he was supposed to be the founding father of the nation. At any rate, the celebration of the anniversary of Hung-Vuong is more of a joyful civic gathering than a religious celebration, as in the case of national hero worship. At least, the spirit of Hung-Vuong I is not believed to have the capability of realizing miracles as effectively as the spirt of Lord Tran or those of the Ladies Trung.

At the present time, religions are not supposed to be repressed. However, religious practices are discouraged and strictly controlled by the government. By contrast, anniversaries of national heroes are still duly celebrated.

Social Structures: The Village

The external appearance of a Vietnamese village is not much different from that of its southern Chinese counterpart. In a

traditional village, which consisted of about 800 to 1,000 inhabitants, the administration was in the hands of a council of notables.
The head of the council was usually the best-educated person in
the village. In theory, education rather than wealth was the only
factor to decide who would be a notable. This was usually the case
before the commercialization of rice production in the village. The
council functioned as a legislative body. The administration was
in the hands of the village chief, or *ly-truong*, who was also a
member of the council. Like the present village revolutionary
committee, the council of notables had full financial, political, and
moral power over the village. In general, the village was the basic
political unit in the Vietnamese society and was treated as such
by the central government. Taxes and military services were
allocated to the villagers by the council itself.

In defending village autonomy against the central government,
village notables frequently pointed out the "constitutional
principle," saying that "village regulations are above royal
decrees." Even though the king had the power to impose his will
on the village, normally he hesitated to do so. In some exceptional
cases, the unwritten constitutional principle about village autonomy was disregarded by the central government. At least on two
occasions, "rebel villages" were completely eradicated from the
map and all their inhabitants were beheaded by the king's
executioner.

According to Confucian principles, villagers were supposed
to respect the notables and obey their orders. However, in practice,
the behaviour of the notables, rather than the teaching of Confucius, was the main factor. It was not rare that a poor and frustrated
peasant would pretend to be drunk and insult the notables, who
could do nothing against him, especially if other villagers were on
his side. This somewhat un-Confucian behaviour was not limited
within the confines of the village. Emperors and ministers were
often ridiculed by stories and actions. Every Vietnamese child
knew the stories of Dr. Pig's stupidity or Dr. Quynh's practical
jokes against the emperor and the prime minister. Chinese
mandarins, French governors general, and recently, American
advisers, Russian comrades, cadres, and even Uncle Ho all shared
the same fate as the Vietnamese emperors of the past: all became
the laughing stock of the people because of their "ignorance" or
"naivety." This deep resentment against authority figures in the
Vietnamese culture was probably the crucial factor helping the

Vietnamese to remain Vietnamese in spite of ruthless Sinification and Westernization imposed on them by their powerful invaders.

In short, the political structure of the village could lend itself easily to dictatorship within the village. Normally, such an abuse of power was restrained by the village traditions. As expected, during the colonial period, these traditional guarantees quickly disappeared in the hands of one or two landlords who were more interested in making money than respecting village traditions. As a result, brutal exploitation in the village not only destroyed the basic structure of the Vietnamese nation but also provided fuel for the socio-political revolution at the present time.

Under the Communist regime, the village is still an important political unit. Administrative autonomy is still usually respected. Of course, unlike the notables of the past, members of the revolutionary committee of the village are selected on the basis of party loyalty and poverty rather than on education or wealth. Political authority given to the village committee covers every aspect of the village life. It is not uncommon that a "traitor," released by the people's court at the provincial level, is ordered to report to his village to be arrested again by the village committee. Provincial or even regional authority cannot do anything against the village revolutionary committee. In other words, the village administration becomes a real dictatorship. At the village level, dictatorship of the proletariat means dictatorship of the party and poor peasants.

Social Structures: The Family

If the village is the basic political unit of the nation, then the family is the basic social unit of the society. The size of a family depends on its wealth. Rich families normally consist of members of three generations — the extended family — who frequently meet with each other, usually at the death anniversary of the ancestors and during the Lunar New Year festival. Normally, both in rich and poor families, one finds only the parents and their young children living under the same roof as in the West. As soon as an individual has set up his family, he moves out of his parents' home if he can find a house in which to settle down. Old parents usually live with the oldest son or the richest son. Regardless of the social status of a family, a child is considered to be the future of the family and even of the nation. For this reason, preschool children are somewhat spoiled by the constant attention of everyone. In return, they are expected to show respect to their elders. Older children are supposed to be responsible for the welfare and even behaviour of their younger brothers and sisters. It is not uncommon to find that a child is reprimanded because his or her younger sibling does not behave properly.

As the future of the family, children — especially of middle-class and upper-class families — are constantly pushed to attain their highest achievements at school. Competitions between children are frequently encouraged. This method of child-rearing practice tends to create social conflicts in the family. As a result, Vietnamese families are less tightly knit than the Chinese or Japanese families. Furthermore, this competitive spirit inculcated during childhood generates a strong achievement orientation in the Vietnamese culture. On the other hand, it does not help the Vietnamese to develop adequate social skills in dealing with each other. Voluntary co-operations among Vietnamese themselves are not very long lasting. They may get together a few times a year to celebrate their festivals, but they do not live together in ethnic ghettos like a "China Town" or "Little Italy." The centrifugal force in the overseas Vietnamese community is so strong that usually rival associations are set up even though they pursue the same social or political goals.

The most distinctive characteristic of the Vietnamese culture in comparison with other East Asian cultures is the active role of the women in the Vietnamese society. In theory, a Vietnamese female is supposed to be as submissive to male authority as her Chinese or Japanese sisters. However, there is a great difference between theory and practice. Vietnamese females — known to be the "home ministers," or *noi-tuong* — are actually on equal footing with their husbands. All important decisions in the family norm-ally involve the participation of both spouses. In the ancient regime, when polygamy was still legal, the husband could not have a second wife without the explicit approval of his first wife. Furthermore, it was not uncommon for a successful business-woman to decide to get a second wife for her husband so that she could spend her full time in the business world.

During the periods of war, the role of the Vietnamese women obviously becomes crucial for the survival of their families and the nation. While their husbands are busy fighting each other or foreign invaders, Vietnamese women are fully in charge of the family and economic production. For example, during the last war, one could find Vietnamese women of South Vietnam involved in all sorts of economic activities, from import-export business to truck driving or general construction.

Conclusion

No other country in the history of mankind has gone through as many wars as Vietnam. The endurance of the Vietnamese people and the resiliency of their culture have saved their country and nation from disappearance. They have shown their ability to adapt very easily to new conditions. Inside Vietnam, they have known how to learn quickly from their more powerful invaders and used the new knowledge to liberate their country. Outside their country, overseas Vietnamese have shown again their ability not only to adapt but also to prosper within a very short time.

The strategic location of Vietnam in Southeast Asia has invited invasions. By fighting for centuries, a war-oriented culture has been created. Such a culture did help the Vietnamese in the past not only to maintain their independence but also to invade others. With the military technology of the modern age, I am not sure whether the Vietnamese society has enough endurance to go through another devastation. At least, the historical mission of the March to the South should not be turned into a "westward march" against Vietnam's neighbours in the name of class struggle. The "military assistance" that Hanoi has given to Kampuchea has generated a tremendous strain inside the Vietnamese political system. We can only hope that the Vietnamese leaders are aware of the sufferings of their people and concentrate on the task of national reconstruction and development, which is a national challenge as honourable as the resistance against five hundred thousand Mongol warriors.

Young Vietnamese girl in refugee camp.

Cambodia

2

Cambodia

by
Robert Garry

Preamble

Cambodia[1] has been very much in the news in recent years. Everyone has heard of the bloody *Khmer Rouge*,[2] the Vietnamese invasion, and the tragic fate of hundreds of thousands of refugees who have fled into Thailand and who now lead a precarious existence in hastily set up camps.

Cambodia is much more than an occupied country, emptied of its inhabitants, and whose very existence is currently at stake. At a time when thousands of refugees have arrived in Canada — people who have known terrible hardships, who have escaped from many perils, who have lost most of their family and all of their material possessions — it is advisable, if we want to welcome them and facilitate their adaptation to the North American way of life, for us to have some knowledge of what Cambodia was: its institutions, population, cultural heritage, and the spiritual and moral values of its people. This knowledge will enable us to understand the Cambodians who have come here, to gauge their hardships, to appreciate and love them as people. From this can grow a mutual confidence that will bring great joy.

This chapter tells of a Cambodia that no longer exists. It tells of the land many of the refugees knew before it was taken over by

---

1.   *Cambodia* is a synonym of *Khmer*. It comes from *Kambuja*, a name designating the descendants of Kambu, the founder of the country. The word *Khmer* refers to the great Khmer empire, which was, in the thirteenth century, one of the most powerful states in Southeast Asia.

2.   The expression *Khmer Rouge* was coined by Prince Sihanouk to designate the Cambodian Communists who had taken to the bush to fight against the regime of Marshal Lon Nol.

the Khmer Rouge, a country where life was pleasant, a country they would never have wanted to leave.

The Land and Its History

Cambodia is a tropical country situated in Southeast Asia in the Indochinese peninsula.[3] Its area is approximately twice that of the state of Maine. It is bounded on the north and northwest by Thailand[4] and Laos, on the south and east by Vietnam, and on the west by the Gulf of Thailand. The centre of the country is covered by a vast plain on which is found the Tonle Sap ("Great Lake"), and through which flow two great rivers, the Mekong, whose source is in China on the high plateaus of Tibet, and the Tonle Sab, which drains the lake. The central plain is surrounded by chains of mountains covered with forests, and plateaus combining forests and vast grasslands. To the west are the Cardomom Mountains, to the north the Dangrek chain, and to the east the Mois Plateau.

Cambodia is under the influence of the monsoons, which from November to May blow out of the northeast, and from June to October, from the southwest. There are, therefore, two seasons: a dry, cool winter, and a very wet and hot summer. In the capital, Phnom Penh, situated on the central plain on the banks of the Mekong, the hottest month is April, with a temperature of 84.2 degrees Fahrenheit, and the "coolest" month December, with 77.7 degrees. The record high and low are 105 and 57 degrees Fahrenheit respectively. Average annual precipitation for Phnom Penh is 57.3 inches, with a maximum of 11.1 inches in October and a minimum of 0.4 inches in February. However, precipitation varies according to altitude and position in relation to the summer monsoon winds. A precipitation of 221 inches has been recorded on the maritime side of the Gulf of Thailand. It is not surprising that this side is covered with extremely dense forest, analogous to that of the Amazon, while on the other side, and on the plateaus of the interior, one finds a clear forest, similar to that of India, and which Rudyard Kipling describes so magnificently in *The Jungle Book*.

---

3.   The Indochinese peninsula, as its name indicates, is situated between India and China.

4.   Before 1939, Thailand was known as Siam. At the beginning of the war, Siam changed its name to Thailand, meaning "country of free men." There was an ulterior political motive, that of bringing under the authority of Bangkok the Lao Thais of Laos, the Thais of North Vietnam, and even those of southern China.

These forests are rich in plant life and abound in animals such as elephants, wild oxen and buffalo, deer, tigers, panthers. The maritime coast of the Gulf of Thailand, 450 kilometres long, is bounded by a mangrove forest teeming with crocodiles. The sea waters are very rich in fish; every year, during the dry season, shoals of migratory fish, called *plathou*, take shelter along the Cambodian coast, where an intensive fishing industry flourishes.

The Cambodian Population

The population of Cambodia cannot be determined with certainty. It was estimated at 8,110,000 by the United Nations Department of Economic and Social Affairs in 1975. This figure is surely exaggerated. It would seem preferable to rely on the 1972 estimate by Jacques Migozzi in his "Étude sur les faits et problèmes de population," published in Paris in 1973, which gives the following figures:

Total population	7,300,000
Khmers	6,200,000
Chinese	450,000
Vietnamese	450,000
Khmer Islam	150,000
Khmer Loeu	50,000

The population of Vietnamese origin was very much affected by the takeover by Marshal Lon Nol on March 18, 1970. It is estimated that 200,000 Vietnamese may have left Cambodia on their own; 100,000 were repatriated by official South Vietnamese organizations; 20,000 were interned in Cambodia. Of the 120,000 remaining, few seem to have survived. The majority of the Khmer Islam were able, it seems, to reach Malaysia, while most of the Khmers of Chinese origin were able to get to China or Southeast Asian countries such as Thailand and Malaysia. The Khmer population may have been reduced by several million as a result of the Khmer Rouge massacres and the large refugee flow to Thailand.

Origins of the Cambodians

The Khmers are the oldest of the peoples of Indochina. They belong to the Mon group, from the borders of Burma and Tibet, and came down into the south of the peninsula around 1500 B.C. The Khmers of that period were farmers practising irrigated rice cultivation, fishing on rivers with harpoon or bone fishhook, and raising oxen and buffalo, which they had succeeded in domesticating. They made stone tools and clay pottery. They had discovered fire and they lived in raised houses. They worshipped their ancestors and the spirits of the earth and the waters, and they venerated the serpent Naga, which symbolized the cosmic forces, and which has remained the guardian spirit of Cambodia and one of the favourite themes of Khmer art.

The Indianization of the Khmer People

In very ancient times, a king, called Kambu, ruled over the region of the Arya in India. Around 50 A.D., one of his descendants, Kaundinya, relinquished the throne and, crossing the seas, disembarked on the shores of the Mekong Delta, which was inhabitated by a Khmer group worshipping the serpent Naga. After repelling the natives who wanted to seize his ship, he met the king of the Naga, with whom he found favour and who gave him the hand of his daughter, Soma. The descendants of Kambu, or Kambuja, gave their name to Kampuchea, anglicized as Cambodia. They brought to the Khmer people a religion, Mahayana Buddhism; a scholarly language, Sanskrit; an Indian alphabet; the laws of India; and, above all, the Hindu conception of the monarchy.

The successors of Kaundinya founded the Kingdom of the Mountain, so called for Mount Meru, the cosmic mountain, the centre of the world. The Chinese called it the Kingdom of Funan. At this time, a further Indianization was brought about by a brahmin of the same clan as the founder of the Kingdom of the Mountain. Brahminism gained new favour with the royal family and the court dignitaries. The political and social organization was modelled on that of the Indian states. The Cambodian rulers developed friendly relations with China and launched an ambitious irrigation program that brought great prosperity to the country. The Chinese ambassadors of the time were particularly struck by the gentleness, the naturalness of the Khmers, and by the humane charity, derived from the Buddhist religion, as practised by the country people.

During the second and third centuries A.D., a Hinduized kingdom, Chenla, was constituted to the west of the middle Mekong. It became quite powerful and took over Funan between 560 and 630 A.D. Extending its hegemony towards the south, it spread its culture and its language, Ancient Khmer, which became in less than two centuries the lingua franca of West Indochina. In the late eighth century, the Chenla king was assassinated and his kingdom, attacked by Javanese pirates, became a vassal of the Sailendra rulers of Java.

Around 800 A.D., Jayavarman, a young Cambodian prince who had been forcibly taken to Java, secretly returned to Cambodia. He subdued, one by one, all the principalities that had become independent, unified the country, broke with Java, and in 899 built the first Angkor to the north of the Great Lake. He made this his capital and here he instituted the worship of the god-king, or Devaraja. Subsequently, statues of successive rulers, bearing the features of the gods of the Brahmin pantheon, were erected (see drawing at introduction to section). One of his successors, Indravarman, gave the royal court the organization it still had on March 18, 1970, when Prince Sihanouk was deposed by Marshal Lon Nol. The son of Indravarman constructed the great reservoir (Baray) and created a large extension of rice cultivation. He was at once a powerful warrior, a great builder, and an excellent administrator. After innumerable political vicissitudes, dynastic quarrels, and a long civil war, Cambodia came under the rule of an usurper, Suryavarman, who came into conflict with his neighbours. During his reign, between 1122 and 1150 the magnificent temple of Angkor Wat was built. And under his successor, Jayavarman VII, Cambodia attained its greatest territorial expansion. Apart from the modern Khmer territory, it included Champa, that is, the whole centre of Vietnam, the present area of South Vietnam, Laos, and Thailand, part of the Malay peninsula as far as the Isthmus of Kra, and part of Lower Burma. It was, after China, the largest and most powerful country of the Far East.

Jayavarman VII was a faithful follower of Mahayana, or Buddhism of the Big Raft. He built the city of Angkor Thom, which he dotted with monuments; the most prestigious is the Bayon, a splendid temple. Anxious to acquire merit for his future life, he built 102 hospitals and numerous rest-houses (*salas*) for travellers. On the stela of Say Fong there is this inscription: "He suffered from the sickness of his subjects more than from his own, for it is public pain which causes pain for kings, and not their own pain."

In the late thirteenth century, Cambodia was attacked by the Thai who, under pressure from the Mongols, had infiltrated the Mekong and Menam valleys. The Khmer people fought against the invaders; after enormous losses and considerable devastation, Cambodia lost its Siamese and Laotian dependencies. The hydraulic network fell into disrepair and agricultural production collapsed, bringing on a general famine, which, combined with the deportation of the civilian population by the Siamese armies, led to a veritable depopulation of the country. In 1351, Angkor was besieged and, after more than a year, fell to the Thai who pillaged it and took its inhabitants as slaves. After a brief respite, due to a Cambodian rebellion led by a brother of the king, the war resumed and continued almost without interruption until 1431. The city of Angkor was besieged once more and 70,000 inhabitants were deported to Siamese territory. In 1432, Angkor was recaptured and its garrison massacred; however, because the city was too vulnerable, the capital was moved to Phnom Penh in 1434. From 1467 to 1529, Cambodia was torn between rival factions. This provided the opportunity for the Siamese to lay hands on certain parts of the Cambodian territory and to demand payment of a tribute. After a victory of the Cambodian troops in 1512 — at a place ever since called Siemreap, or the crushing of the Siamese — the Cambodian king built a capital to the south of Phnom Penh, where it would be safe from enemy forays.

The Europeans in Cambodia

The first European to set foot in Cambodia was the Portuguese Dominican Gaspar Da Cruz, who arrived in 1555 with the intention of evangelizing the country. He stayed only a short time and returned to Malacca (in present-day Malaysia). A few years later, the conflict with Siam had resumed and the Cambodians faced an attack of 100,000 Siamese who seized the provinces of Battambang and Pursat and advanced to lay siege to the capital. The Cambodian king appealed to the Portuguese and the Spanish, and a Portuguese adventurer, Diego Veloso, assembled a few soldiers and came to Cambodia in 1594. Veloso and his companions were captured by the Siamese and sent back to the Philippines with the assignment of negotiating an alliance for the Siamese with the Spanish. They returned to Cambodia with warships and soldiers and drove out the usurpers, who had installed themselves on the throne with the aid of the Siamese, and restored the legitimate royal authority. Throughout the seventeenth century, Portuguese and Spaniards settled in Cambodia and enjoyed the support of Cambodian rulers. Many of them married local women, and their descendants are today authentic Cambodians, despite foreign names such as Montana, Pitou de Monteiro, or De Lopez.

Relations Between Cambodia and Vietnam

In the early seventeenth century, the Cambodian king recognized Siamese overlordship, and there was a violent reaction. The king was dethroned and a new ruler restored Khmer independence in 1618, refused to pay tribute to Siam, and established his capital at Oudang, where it remained until 1867. To counterbalance the Siamese influence, King Chey Chetta, who had married a Vietnamese princess, sought support from Vietnam, ruled by the Nguyen family. Vietnam had conquered the kingdom of Champa in 1471 and found itself on the borders of the southern Cambodian provinces. With the agreement of the Khmer ruler, Vietnamese settlements were founded in Cambodian territory. Vietnam then imposed the payment of tribute on the Cambodian government and successfully claimed the lands occupied by its nationals. From this time on, caught in a stranglehold between Vietnamese and Siamese, Cambodia helplessly witnessed the systematic dismemberment of its territory. It was alternately the vassal of Siam and of Vietnam and had to give up part of its best lands to each of its successive protectors.

In 1834, the Vietnamese embarked on a systematic Vietnamization of the Khmer people, in an attempt to destroy their language, traditions, and religion. In 1841 came annexation, and Cambodia ceased to exist. It became Vietnamese territory. However, in 1845, aided by the Siamese, the Cambodian population rose up and drove out the Vietnamese. Siam kept all the Cambodian provinces, which it had occupied for fifty years, while Vietnam permanently annexed the southern part of present-day South Vietnam. Convinced that sooner or later Cambodia was bound to be divided up between Vietnam and Siam, King Ang Duong in 1855 sent a letter to Napoleon III soliciting French protection. The protectorate treaty was signed in July, 1863. King Norodom, the son of Ang Duong, was ceremonially crowned at Phnom Penh on June 3, 1864, in the presence of French and Siamese representatives.

The French Protectorate and the Independence Period

As a result of difficulties created by court mandarins and ladies, a rebellion broke out against the royal authority in 1884. It ceased in 1887 when the French government gave back to the king of Cambodia his complete authority and restored a regime of indirect administration. By the treaties of 1904 and 1907, Cambodia regained the provinces of Battambang and of Siemreap, as well as the territories situated to the south of the Dangrek chain, which Siam had annexed.

During the two world wars, Cambodia was governed with foresight and acquired an important economic infrastructure of rubber plantations, an admirable road network, a railway line into Thailand, and the maritime port of Kompong Som, which was developed under Norodom Sihanouk. Great efforts were made in education resulting in huge increases in the number of pagoda and Pali schools, the setting up of secondary schools in the major inland cities, and of a royal university in Phnom Penh. Cultural achievements were just as impressive. These included the creation of the National Museum at Phnom Penh, the restoration of the monuments at Angkor and of the royal mausoleums at Oudong, publications by the Buddhist Institute, several successful campaigns for the development of education, and the reassertion of the value of manual labour among the educated.

After gaining independence in 1953, Sihanouk drew closer to China, with which he signed a friendship and non-aggression treaty in 1960, and denounced, vigorously, the implantation of Vietnamese Communists in Cambodia. In early 1970, Sinanouk went to the Soviet Union and China to solicit their intervention against Hanoi, with a view to stopping Communist forays into Cambodia.

During his absence, Sihanouk was deposed by Prime Minister Lon Nol, on March 18, 1970. Events now moved quickly. The prince took refuge in Peking and founded the Gouvernement Royal d'Union Nationale Khmère (GRUNK). This received the immediate, enthusiastic support of the Khmer Communist resistance fighters, led by Khieu Samphan, who were fighting against the Khmer Republic founded by Lon Nol. On May 1, 1970, Cambodia was invaded by South Vietnamese troops, supported by the U.S. Air Force, which bombed the country savagely and indiscriminately. The struggle between the Communist resistance fighters, called the Khmer Rouge by Sihanouk, and Lon Nol's republican troops became more intense, ending with the victory of the former, who entered Phnom Penh on April 17, 1975. Prince Sihanouk returned from Peking to Phnom Penh on September 9. He was maintained in his office as head of state but had no real power. Shortly afterwards, he left for Paris and New York, where at the United

Nations he defined the non-alignment policy of Cambodia. He returned to Phnom Penh and presided over the Council of Ministers, which, on January 9, 1976, ratified the new constitution proclaiming the Democratic State of Cambodia and created a People's Assembly elected by universal suffrage. Prince Sihanouk was a candidate in the capital in the election of March 20, 1976, and received 100 percent of the votes. He was chosen unanimously by the assembly to be head of state. Considering that his role was over, and that he could not associate himself with the policies being implemented by the government of Democratic Kampuchea, Sihanouk resigned from his office as head of state on April 2, 1976. He was then confined to the Khemarin Palace in Phnom Penh, which he did not leave until January 6, 1979. Liberated by the Khmer Rouge the day before the Vietnamese army entered Phnom Penh, he boarded a Chinese plane with his suite and flew to Peking.

The Khmer Rouge had openly fought the Vietnamese for over a year. In the summer of 1978, 70,000 Vietnamese troops had invaded Cambodia and, in a few days, occupied large portions of Khmer territory. On Christmas Eve, 100,000 Vietnamese troops, supported by tanks, artillery, and aircraft, swept into Cambodia. Phnom Penh, deserted by the Khmer Rouge, was occupied on January 7, 1979. A pro-Vietnamese regime, headed by Colonel Heng Samrin, the former president of the Revolutionary Council of Democratic Kampuchea, was installed in Phnom Penh. The Khmer Rouge took to the bush and organized pockets of resistance in the Cardamoms to the southwest.

Prince Sihanouk went to New York and denounced the Vietnamese aggression before the UN Security Council, but at the same time, he condemned the crimes of Pol Pot and his friends and tabled a resolution enjoining the evacuation of the Vietnamese troops. This was vetoed by the Soviet Union. The prince, from his refuge in Peking, suggested that all sides concerned, and the members of the Association of Southeast Asian Nations (ASEAN), should participate in a conference in Geneva on Indochina, which would permit a ceasefire in Cambodia and the holding of free elections under UN supervision. This proposal was not followed up. On November 14, 1979, the UN General Assembly — by 104 votes to 21, with 21 abstentions — passed a resolution demanding the withdrawal of foreign troops from Cambodia. This resolution has gone unheeded, and the war has continued between the Khmer

Rouge and the Vietnamese troops, while Cambodia is steadily drained of its inhabitants.

The Cambodian Refugees

Despite the wall of silence and secrecy erected by the Pol Pot regime, the world has learned of the terrible fate of the Cambodian people through accounts by the refugees and resistance groups hiding in the jungle. Massacres, executions, forced labour, deportation, imprisonment — these have been their daily lot. All potential opponents, whether they collaborated with Sihanouk, Lon Nol, or the Americans, have been liquidated. All the educated, all those who have studied abroad, or who have a veneer of Western culture, have been shot or sent to forced labour camps from which few return. Several million Cambodians have perished at the hands of the Khmer Rouge or en route to exile. The situation in Cambodia is dramatic: generalized starvation; abominable public health, which cannot be improved for lack of doctors and medicine; sterility among women; high infant mortality; and, everywhere, hordes of runaways trying to reach Thailand and deserting the young, the old, and the sick who are unable to continue. Over a million refugees are now in camps in Thailand or near the border of Cambodia. Thanks to international aid and the dedication of UNICEF and International Red Cross personnel, their basic needs are being met; most are waiting for a host country to agree to take them in; many others are hoping that the situation in Cambodia will improve and that they will be able to return home. None of them can forget that Cambodia was a haven of peace, where life was pleasant. A glimpse of this life follows.

The Traditional Khmer Way of Life

Crops

Cambodians are above all farmers. Irrigated rice cultivation is their principal activity and chief concern. This is not intensive and exclusive, occupying all the land and seeking a maximum yield. There is plenty of room in Cambodia; the population is relatively small. Thus, there is a great deal of unoccupied arable land. The Cambodian peasant is not a painstaking farmer. He rarely uses fertilizer and usually harvests only one crop a year. In the lowlands and around the Tonle Sap, irrigated rice cultivation is carried on. The rice grows as the flooding increases and it is harvested by *pirogue*, or piragua, a canoe made from a single tree trunk.

Besides rice, the peasants grow, on the rich land of the river-banks, maize, cotton, mulberries, vegetables, and fruits such as the mango, sweetsop, litchi, longan, guava, mangosteen, durian, and coconut. There are also commercial crops, including hevea, pepper, and tobacco. Along the fields stand the sugar palms, providential trees providing sugar, palm wine, and building materials.

Livestock

The Cambodian is also adept at livestock breeding. There is no family that does not own a few oxen or buffalo for working the land. The latter are raised in almost complete freedom, for they are able to defend themselves against predators. Oxen are generally penned under the house at night and graze nearby during the day, watched over by young herdsmen. As a rule, Cambodians raise neither hogs nor fowl, for killing a living creature is the greatest sin a Buddhist can commit. However, some raise roosters for cock-fighting, a popular sport.

In the Cardamoms, the Cambodians capture and train elephants. These are then given identity cards and are sometimes sold to Thais or Burmese for use in the teak forests in the north of their countries.

Fish

The Cambodians consume very little or no meat and find in fish, molluscs, and crustaceans the protein, fat, and mineral salts they require. They fish on the smallest streams, in lakes, and along the seacoast. They fish for their families and themselves. The Cambodian waters are extremely rich in fish. During the rainy season, the Tonle Sap receives the waters of the Mekong; the lake triples its area and floods the neighbouring forests. This provides rich and varied food for fish, which grow extremely fast. During the full moon of November, when the current reverses and the waters of the lake start to flow back towards the Mekong, the aquatic life, as if moved by an instinct of self-preservation, hurries downstream. This is the time for fishing. (The sites used to be leased out to Chinese, who employed a largely Vietnamese labour force.) Enormous dams of tree trunks and wicker are built across the river, while artificial groves made from tree branches lure the fish to easy capture. The fishing is truly extraordinary.

The Cambodian peasants go to the fishing sites where they exchange rice, vegetables, and fruit for fish, which they use to make the *prahoc*, or fish paste, the national condiment consumed with rice. During the dry season, veritable caravans of carts pulled by oxen or buffalo can be seen making their way to the Great Lake. The prahoc is prepared on the spot. The fish head, scales, and insides are removed. Then the fish are washed, salted, dried, ground, reduced to a pulp, and put out to ferment in the sun in large covered jars. The juice that appears on the surface is the *tuktrey*, or Cambodian brine. The fish caught on the shores of the Gulf of Thailand are dried, salted, and sent to the plantations of Southeast Asia where they become food for the plantation labourers.

Transportation

When Cambodians travel, it is generally by using animals. Horse-drawn vehicles are rare, but every family has an ox or buffalo cart, which is used in the dry season particularly. During the rainy season, the most common means of transportation is the pirogue. In the mountains and forests, where there are no communication routes, the elephant is the only way to move about and is, therefore, extremely valuable.

Land Tenure

In Cambodia, large estates are rare and have usually been constituted by dignitaries who receive a concession from the king, or who accumulated funds while carrying out their duties. The principal source of labour for the large landowners is the practice of usury. The interest rates are high, reaching 100 percent a year, and occasionally exceeding that. Insolvent peasants are hired to pay off their debts and lose the use, even the ownership, of their lands. But as a general rule, the soil is exploited by small landowners and their families, without salaried labour. Mutual aid among villages is common and the rural population, while living modestly, never knew either hunger or poverty until recent developments. Ownership can be acquired through the continuous exploitation of the land and the payment of the property tax for five consecutive years. Occupancy is established by the registry service and leads to the issue of a title deed.

Industry

Cambodia possesses no industries outside those set up through Chinese or French aid — cotton and jute mills, plywood and paper mills, oil refineries. On the other hand, Cambodians make for themselves everything necessary for everyday life; that is, their houses, carts, pirogues, clothing. The only craftsmen engaged by the Cambodian peasant are potters, blacksmiths, and the jewellers and silversmiths to whom he turns for the small objects that embellish his life and represent his savings. Bracelets, necklaces, ear-rings, bowls, cups, and betel services are some of these ornaments.

Cambodia has no important mining resources, although there are a few meagre iron deposits, a few sapphires and rubies, and marble quarries at Pursat and a little jet in the Cardamoms.

Diet

The principal food of the Cambodians is rice, to which are added the prahoc, dried fish, shrimp paste, and occasionally brine. Meat consumption is practically nil in the country and very low in the cities, for, as Buddhists, the Cambodians abstain from slaughtering animals. The cuisine is extremely refined and complex: that is why housewives prefer to serve Chinese or French dishes to their guests. A great variety of tasty fruits is eaten. The most common drink is pure water; occasionally, palm wine made from the fermented sap of the sugar palm is consumed. A number of Cambodians have recently begun to drink tea and coffee, and in the orchards of the southwest, some tea and coffee is grown.

Dress

Cambodia belongs to the group of countries of Indian civilization whose inhabitants wear draped clothes. The typical costume is the *sampot*, a piece of cotton or silk wrapped around the waist and with the longest piece brought between the legs and attached behind at the waist. The sampot looks something like a pair of puffed-out pants. Worn especially by men, the sampot has recently become a ceremonial costume. Women mostly wear the Malay *sarong*, a simple piece of material wrapped around the waist, to which is added the short-sleeved bolero that conceals their chests. In the remote inland regions, many women used to go bare-breasted. More and more country people, both men and women, now wear black trousers and a close-fitting top. Both use a piece of material or a towel tied in front, in the shape of a turban for men, and loosely for women. But most men go bare-headed. While men and women used to have crew cuts, this style is on the wane.

The House

The Cambodian house faces the rising sun. It is rectangular and sits on high posts. Among the poor, it has a single room; among the wealthier, there is a division into one or two extra rooms by means of partitions of dried, plaited palm leaves.

Behind the house, and separated from it to avoid fires, stands a small shed serving as a kitchen. The house is made entirely of vegetable matter: the columns are hardwood, which is rotproof and termite-resistant; the walls, partitions, and roof are dried palm leaves; the floors are bamboo or split palm tree trunks. Under the house, the cart, the pirogue, and the loom are stored. There is a small pen for animals. The house is sparsely furnished — a few mats, some small kapok cushions, a jewel chest and silk sampots, a betel service, silver or copper bowls, wooden trays, pots, and an earth stove.

Building a house, buying a buffalo, and taking a wife are, it is said, the three most serious acts in life. That is why strict rites preside over the construction of a house. The *achar*, or seer of the nearest Buddhist pagoda, determines the date and time for beginning the work with reference to the day and hour of the owner's birth. Hardwood trees have been selected in the forest. They will be cut down and transported to the construction site and implanted at a date set by the achar, who will personally preside over the ceremonious installation of the master beam and the sacrifices to the spirits of the earth. When the house is completed, the family enters, at a date and time set by the achar, and invoking the protection of Buddha.

Cambodians are individualists and, unlike the Vietnamese and Chinese, do not gather in villages. The Cambodian village is, so to speak, non-existent; it is made up of dwellings scattered in sugar palm groves or in the ricefields; it is a collection of tiny hamlets each of which often has a single family.

The Cities

The majority of the Cambodian population is rural. The cities are predominantly Chinese or Vietnamese, with the Cambodian population gathering on the periphery near the countryside and living in raised houses. The Chinese and Vietnamese are concentrated around the market in "compartments" of one or two storeys, with shops on the ground floor and offices and living quarters above. Phnom Penh had barely 200,000 inhabitants. Its population increased rapidly in the seventies, as the countryside was abandoned, and reached 2.5 million in 1974. The city was emptied by the Khmer Rouge in April, 1975, and is now a ghost town with abandoned houses, overrun by vegetation. Its population may now number only in the tens of thousands. The other cities, which played the role of provincial capitals, were much smaller; Battambang had 150,000 and Kompong Cham, 90,000. We have no information on their present populations.

Cambodian Society

Cambodian society is a free society where the individual is not subordinate to his family or social group, as among the Chinese or Vietnamese. However, there was no escape from the exactions of mandarins, or from the constraints imposed by Vietnamese and Siamese invaders before the French Protectorate. Living in a sparsely populated country with abundant resources, the Cambodians were not much pressed by need. They enjoyed life and devoted their plentiful leisure time to music, dance, and theatre — arts in which they are quite talented.

Buddhism has given to Cambodian society not only its gentleness, peace, and charity, but also a certain indifference to those material goods that could be obtained through more active ambition.

Cambodians today retain a few primitive animistic beliefs and some remnants of shamanism or Brahminism, which had survived until recent years in the rites of the Royal Palace and had been preserved by the *bakus*, descendants of ancient brahmins.

Family Organization

Cambodian society is patriarchal. The father is the head of the family, but he is not all-powerful. The rights he possesses over his wife and children are counterbalanced by duties prescribed by Buddhist morality and sanctioned by civil law. The children live without restraint in the family home. When they marry, they are emancipated ipso facto and go to live in a separate house, without having to ask the authorization of their parents to leave. The marriage proposal is made by intermediaries sent by the parents of the young man, while an old man of recognized wisdom plays this role for the young woman and attends all ceremonies. The date of the wedding is determined by the achar, with reference to the birth signs of the couple. During the engagement period, which can last two years, the financés parents must bring presents to the parents of the bride-to-be twice a month. (Not so long ago, the fiancé went to "act the son-in-law" in the house of his future parents-in-law as soon as the engagement ceremony was celebrated. He stayed there until the wedding.) A few days before the wedding, the young man and his family build a reception shed and a smaller building that will be used as a kitchen. The revelling lasts two days, and guests make a payment to cover the cost of the banquet. This they will, of course, get back when they themselves marry off one of their children.

The wedding lasts three days. It begins with the payment of the money demanded by the bride's parents and continues with various ceremonies, carried on in the presence of the monks of the pagoda, who recite prayers. The achar is the master of ceremonies and attends to the performance of the rites. Family structure is based on the couple, and relationship does not go beyond the fourth collateral degree. The young man no longer belongs to his own family with the conclusion of the engagement. After marriage, the couple live in a house built near that of the bride's parents. Polygamy is allowed but is rarely practised, except in wealthy families where the husband can afford to support several wives. Cambodian marriages are generally solid; if the husband falls in love with another woman, he prefers divorce over bringing her into the home as a concubine.

The rights of the husband vis-à-vis his wife are strictly limited. He cannot undertake any important action without her consent. He cannot sell his wife, sell himself, put up financial backing, or become a *bonze* (Buddhist monk) in a monastery. The wife does not stay in the background, especially if she has held her head a little higher than her husband during certain marriage ceremonies and thus demonstrated her authority in advance. In the event of divorce, which can be requested by either spouse, the goods acquired during marriage are divided, the husband receiving two-thirds, the wife one-third.

Religious Structure

Theravada Buddhism

Hinayana Buddhism, or Buddhism of the Little Raft, better known in Cambodia as Theravada, is the state religion. It coexisted for a long period with Brahminism and Mahayana Buddhism, but these have now all but disappeared. Buddhism is not a revealed dogma, but rather a way, a line of conduct, a psychological attitude that gives direction to one's life. The sacred writings of Theravada, considered as Orthodox Buddhism, are written in the Pali language and are called Tripitaka, "The Three Collections." The first deals with monastic discipline; the second deals with general religious questions; the third, with morality and philosophy. The community of monks, or bonzes, constitutes the Sangha. The bonzes are not priests; they only rarely take final vows and can leave their monastery and yellow robes behind whenever they so desire. For the duration of his stay in a monastery, a Buddhist monk takes vows of poverty, chastity, and non-violence towards all living beings.

Religious teachings, through the telling of the former lives of Buddha, "Jatakas," permeate all life in Cambodia. From this the Khmers derive their respect for life in all its forms, their tolerance, honesty, frankness. The Buddhist monks, moreover, have played an important role in the progress of the nation, particularly in education and public health.

The Buddhist clergy is entirely independent of the civil authority. The king intervened only as a defender of the faith and to appoint religious dignitaries. The monks belong to two different orders: the Mohanikay, the most popular and ancient, is especially prevalent in the countryside; the Thommayut is more aristocratic and more recent, dating from 1864. To the latter belong most of the monks of the capital and the larger cities. Each order has its own head, chosen by the king from among the highest dignitaries of the clergy.

The monasteries where the monks live are called *wats*, or pagodas in the West. The monastery comprises the shrine proper, or Vihara, where the statue of Buddha is located, and various buildings called *salas*, for the use of visitors, and also used for the pagoda school and for prayer and meditation. All around, scattered among the trees, are small raised huts called *cots*; these are the monks' dwellings. In each wat is found a pond where lotuses grow and a holy tree, the "Ficus religiosis," which recall Buddha's enlightenment. Each monastery is headed by a *chau athicar*, who watches over the monks and the novices and pupils at the pagoda school. A lay person called achar, as noted, is a sort of seer who participates in the lay and religious ceremonies, manages the affairs of the monastery, and maintains the relations of the monks with the population and the government. Primary education is dispensed by teaching bonzes. Classes are held only in the morning, for three years. In 1961, there were 12,000 pupils, attending 590 pagoda schools. As of January 1, 1967, Cambodia had 61,014 bonzes belonging to 3,153 monasteries, of which 2,853 were Mohanikay and 320, Thommayut.

Islam in Cambodia

Islam is practised by the Khmer Islam, descended from the Cham immigrants and Indonesian Malays. In 1970, they numbered over 100,000. They are all Sunni Moslems. In their mosques, the religious community is under an *hakem*. *Imams* preside over the five daily prayers and the ritual prostrations, while *katips* attend to preaching from the Koran. Every year, there are Khmer Islam who go on the pilgrimage to Mecca. Others content themselves with Koranic teaching at Kelantan in Malaysia.

Mahayana Buddhism

The Chinese community, and part of the Vietnamese community, belong to Mahayana Buddhism, strongly tinged with Taoist practices. The Chinese and Vietnamese monks are often seers, or healers, and play an important role in orienting the soul of their faithful at death. Most of the monasteries are at Phnom Penh and in the large inland towns.

Christianity

Christianity is represented especially by the Roman Catholic Church, whose adherents were Occidentals and Vietnamese. Phnom Penh had a bishop and possessed a cathedral and several churches. The majority of the faithful were concentrated in a special district, called the "Catholic village," and in a parish on the Chrui-Changvar peninsula between the Tonle Sap and the Mekong. No Cambodian had become a Christian.

Religious and Secular Holidays

Cambodian holidays are common and popular. They all bear the stamp of religion and their secular side is only superficial. These are some of the best known.

The New Year (Cul Chnam Tigey)

The Khmer New Year is celebrated on April 12 or 13. It marks the beginning of the solar year and is accompanied by the erection of small piles of sand, representing the great mountains of the Hindu cosmogony, dominated by Mount Meru, the axis of the world. This ceremony was formerly celebrated inside the Silver Pagoda in the Royal Palace of Phnom Penh, in the Buddhist monasteries, and also in the humblest of homes. In the villages, traditional games, dancing, and singing are organized and the whole population rejoices.

The Sacred Furrow

This celebration takes place in the spring, in April or May. It is a fertility rite and also the signal for the beginning of work in the fields. Formerly, the king traced the first furrows in a sacred ricefield of the capital, and the queen threw rice seed in the air. During the ceremony, the bakus invoke the protection of the gods for the upcoming harvests. The sacred oxen are unhitched at the end of the ceremony and led to silver trays containing rice, maize, beans, water, sesame, grass, and rice alcohol. From their choice are derived omens for the harvests.

The Triple Anniversary of Buddha

This three-feast ceremony is, above all, religious. It comme-morates the birth, enlightenment, and death of Buddha. It is one of the most important religious holidays of the year and is observed in all monasteries in May.

The Feast of the Dead lasts two weeks and takes place in August and September. It is celebrated in every pagoda, ending with a banquet in honour of the spirits of ancestors and departed friends who have returned to the living for those few days. On the last day, cakes and various offerings are placed in a hollowed-out banana tree trunk, which is floated down a river and is supposed to accompany the spirits to their dwelling-place.

The Feast of the Waters and Salutations to the Moon is the greatest traditional holiday and also the most spectacular. It takes place on a day of the full moon in November and marks the annual flooding, the reversing of the current of the Tonle Sab, and the departure of the fish of the Great Lake for the sea. In Phnom Penh, the king went to his floating house for three days. Every afternoon there were pirogue races and parades of richly decorated and illuminated junks. This holiday corresponds to the return of the fertilizing Naga serpents to the riverbeds, a poetic evocation of the bounty of the rising water.

The Feast of the Offering to the Monks (Katchen) is celebrated every year in September. It is a demonstration of piety on the part of the faithful to gain merit for a future life, by offering to the monks clothes and various objects useful to the community. It is accompanied by prayers and sermons before the statue of Buddha in the monastery shrine. The celebration ends with secular festivities — music, dancing, theatre, and singing.

The Cambodia of Tomorrow

Even a basic study of the present regime in Cambodia is beyond the scope of this chapter. However, we can try to imagine, in the light of past history and present developments, just what lies in store for Cambodia.

The legal government of Cambodia, in the eyes of the international community, is at present Democratic Kampuchea. It is run by a handful of guerrillas under the authority of Khieu Samphan and Pol Pot, openly fighting against the Vietnamese army of occupation from their bases in the Cardamom forests. Democratic Kampuchea is supported by the People's Republic of China and, to a certain extent, by Thailand, which see in it the last bulwark against Vietnamese hegemonism, the latter supported by the Soviet Union.

In Phnom Penh there is a puppet government, set up by the Vietnamese and headed by a former Khmer Rouge renegade, Colonel Heng Samrin, who claims to represent the sole legal authority in Cambodia. The Vietnamese recently decided that this situation, which they have created, is irreversible, and there is thus an impasse. It is not easy to see how Cambodia could regain peace and stability without external intervention. It seems that the only solution resides in the simultaneous withdrawal of Vietnamese and Khmer Rouge forces from the Cambodian scene, with a new provisional government then to be set up by the United Nations in order to bring peace, restore the administration, and organize free elections under international supervision. In this way, a government truly representative of the Cambodian people could be elected. This government would have to be headed by a known and respected Cambodian figure, who would ensure the transition to a new, democratically elected government. This could be Prince Sihanouk, whose charisma has been well demonstrated, or his former minister, Son Sann, who is currently in

Cambodia at the head of the Kampuchean Liberation Front and is taking an active part in the anti-Vietnamese struggle.

Formerly, a popular prophecy in Cambodia concerned the impending disappearance of the Khmer country. The Cambodians said that the Second World War, the Japanese occupation, the overthrow of Prince Sihanouk in 1970, the Khmer Rouge victory of 1975, and finally the Vietnamese invasion of 1979 were only stages in this inevitable decline. Just as in 1863, in a similarly perilous situation, French intervention stopped the downward turn of events for Cambodia vis-à-vis its neighbours, it can be supposed that the intervention of the international community could, once more, ensure the survival of this unhappy country. Let us pray that the *Teuodas*, the protectors of the world, will come once more to the salvation of the Khmer country and its people.

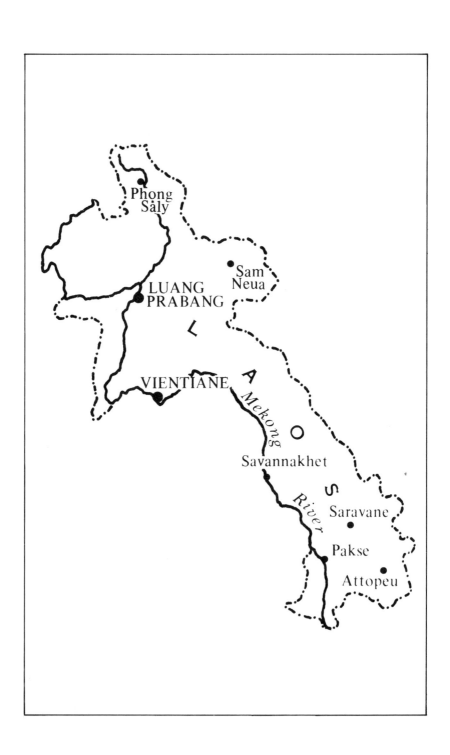

3

Laos:
"The Prince and
the Barb"

by
Peter Royle

An old Lao legend tells of the son and heir apparent of a king of ancient times. Now the king was at war, and an enemy lord was attempting to depose him and place himself on the throne. This lord had a beautiful daughter, with whom the king's son, the Prince, fell in love. The king ordered the prince to stay away from the lord's daughter, as she would only cause him harm. However, the Prince was in love, and disobeying his father, he secretly married her.

Because of the war, it happened that the princess became involved in a plot to murder her husband. She tried to save him from the assassins, but her warnings came too late, and he was hit by a poisoned dart. Fortunately, the poison was not strong enough to kill him, but it did cause him to be dreadfully sick, so that it seemed he had died. He lay for a long time in a coma. During that time, the king became ill and eventually died, passing the throne to his son. By now, the Prince was slowly recovering.

When he was well, preparations were begun for his coronation. The people were happy that good fortune smiled on the Prince, and on them.

But the curse of the poison was still in his blood. A few days before he was to be crowned, the poison acted upon him, and he fell grievously ill. Again, it was thought that he would die, and again he lay for a long time in a coma. Eventually, be began slowly to recover.

Since then, the cycle has continued. The Prince recovers and slowly gets better. Just as it seems that he is at last in perfect health, the poison strikes him down and brings him again to death's door. Suffering is his lot; hope is never completely realized; the curse always prevents him from being crowned.

So it is with his people, whose fortunes follow those of the Prince. Just when it seems that the rains are good, the rice is sufficient, the rivers are full of fish, and they can hope to live in peace, disaster strikes in the forms of famine, war, or oppression.

The Prince has been ill now for some time.

* * * *

Since the mid-seventies, the monsoon rains in Laos have been unusually irregular. People, all the people, have had to dig irrigation ditches by hand in an attempt to get water into the fields to soften the clay, which bakes solid, like pottery, under the kiln-heat of the sun in the long dry season. Under the blistering heat, the rice seedlings in the nurseries grow sickly and weak. Breaking the clay into powder is back-breaking labour, and daily everyone looks up into the burning sky waiting for the rains. Days lengthen into weeks, and still no rain. Insects come to plague the seedlings, even before they are transplanted. Fields that should be glowing with light green shoots in countless rows in countless *padis* lie dry, brown, dead, except for the voracious insects.

Then the rain comes. The skies open and the skies give the rain. The rain settles the five-month curtain of dust. The rain washes your head, face, back, legs, feet, body in a few minutes; but you are not cold. The rain continues, a heavy, drenching rain. It stops. The sun comes out. Everything sparkles. You are happy for the rain. And so is the land. The streams and rivers swell, the banks overflow, the fields begin to turn green.

The rain continues on into November and December — a few minutes or so, an hour or two, every day or most days. All is as it should be. But for the last few years now, the rains have continued past their normal time, and the gently rising water has become deeper and deeper in the rice padis, and the already too-short and weakened stems cannot hold the rice heads above the water. They can survive a few days, but then they begin to drown.

There are many complex causes of the current crisis in Indochina. But the uncertainty of the monsoons, and the consequent shortages in the basic food of the people, would give rise to major problems under any circumstances. Combined with all the other convolutions resulting from decades of foreign and civil wars on the land, major population shifts, profound political and economic upheavals, and the other misfortunes of those tortured countries, it is not easy to dismiss lightly the ancient story of the prince and the curse of the poisoned barb.

Family, Wat, and Village

Like all Southeast Asian countries, Laos is an agricultural country, and the majority of the people live in small rural villages. There are few large towns, and except for Vientiane, the towns are rather more large villages than they are cities. Even Vientiane is essentially a collection of villages that have gradually expanded into each other, and their integral villageness is still the internal dynamic force for the score or so segments that constitute Vientiane.

In the village, daily life centres around the family, which, in terms of survival, depends on the fields, the river, the animals, the jungle. In terms of the village itself, daily life is based in the *wat*. The wat is the Buddhist temple.

Each wat has a number of monks living in it. These monks may often, although not necessarily, be men of the village. There are no priests in Buddhism (that is, trained, professional religious leaders, such as there are in Western religions); there are only monks and devout lay people.

One who enters the monkhood can do so for any length of time, from a few days to a lifetime.[1] Since considerable merit

---

1. Any man may ask the monks in a wat brotherhood if he can join them. Indeed, there is no conversion to Buddhism in the sense of "conversion" or "joining" in Western religions. To be a Buddhist is not a requirement. In fact, a man may be a non-Buddhist and spend his lifetime in a wat. A monk must have severed any and all relationships with the world, including family and personal possessions. This is symbolized by shaving the head and taking the saffron robes of the monk. Even those robes do not belong to the monk. No monk is ever asked for, nor does he ever give any promise of a commitment to, a specific time period that he will remain in the brotherhood of monks. He is free to leave at any time.

accrues to one who enters the monkhood, almost every man has spent a greater or lesser period of time in the wat.

Before widespread Western influence, the wat served as the village school. The children could attend daily classes or stay in the wat as novices. Every wat usually had several young novices as well as the monks.

But this kind of description may already be misleading, for, with our Western orientation, we tend to compartmentalize the different aspects of our lives. Thus far, then, we may be thinking of the wat as being like a church and, in a sense, that is true; for the monks live in the wat, and people pray at the wat. But it also serves as a kind of community centre. So if there is a *boun* ("festival") — like New Year, or the Rocket Festival, or the village boun — it usually finds its centre at the wat. If a travelling troubador comes around, or a company of players, or a film, the activity takes place in the wat. Since the 1975 revolution, the wat has also been the place for the revolutionary seminars, the meetings of the patriotic youth, the village revolutionary council, the literacy classes, and so on.

It is important to understand the profound sense of family and community as a stable and integrated whole. In the predominantly rural, relatively static Lao society, the individual is often seen in relation to the others around him (see Van Esterik, chapter 10). For example, there are separate words in the Lao language for each person in the family: older brother, older sister, younger brother, younger sister, father's older and younger brothers and sisters, mother's older and younger brothers and sisters, grandparents, in-laws, and so on. And in each case, the individual refers to each of these other people by that special relationship title.

There is also a language of respect, a language of common politeness, and a language that is used only by intimate family and friends. These and many other conscious and unconscious habits, rituals, and practices emphasize the security one has in the familiar and known surroundings of a lifetime.

This is significantly different from the experience of many Canadians, for in our industrialized, mobile, technological society, independence is considered very important if an individual is to survive and to do well. We start teaching this when children are very young. Some people, for example, feel that we should let a crying baby cry, for fear of spoiling it with too much attention. We have small families: two parents (or, increasingly, a single parent) with only one, two, or three children. We leave young children in the care of strangers in day-care centres or kindergarten, and then send them to more strangers for public school. Ambition, goal-orientation, competition, aggressiveness — these are encouraged so that our children are formed into individuals who feel that they must depend, as much as possible, on their own resources when they leave home at seventeen or eighteen or nineteen.

In Canada, newly-weds set themselves up on their own; they want to and we feel that they should. But in Laos, the newly-wed groom moves in with his wife's family. There a bride is still her mother's daughter, and her mother, sisters, and other relatives all can help her in her new role of wife and, in due course, young mother. This is unlike Vietnam or some other Asian societies where the newly-weds move in with the groom's family. The Lao feel that this would be very hard on a new bride, who may have to compete with her husband's mother; or, as sometimes happens, she becomes a virtual slave to the mother-in-law.

The groom usually fits into his wife's family quite easily. The marriage probably was, after all, worked out in advance by the elders of both families. The original choice may easily be that of the bride and groom. But it can easily be the choice of the parents too. In either case, the young people and older people all agree together first. Often, the groom knows his bride's family, as the families are likely to be friends already.

In Canada, when someone has a problem, it is up to the person involved to try to solve it by himself. Often the need to seek advice is seen or felt to be a kind of weakness, so we tend to try to be completely self-reliant. If we do need help, we often go to a professional who is objective, neutral, detached, a stranger — and, of course, paid.

In Laos, solutions to problems are usually sought within the family, for that is what families are for. In the family there is no particular memory of credits and debits; the family simply deals with individual needs as they arise. Of course, being a family member has its responsibilities. Thus, if you can be the one to respond to another family member's need, you do, for you expect no more or less of other family members.

We Canadians, therefore, need to understand that for a Lao there is a deep and profound attachment to the home, the family, and the home village. For whatever reason, to leave all of that forever — the relatives, the lifelong friends, the land, the river, the village — is traumatic, world-shattering.

Some people, especially those who are sponsoring refugees, have already had the experience of a newcomer sitting in the midst of a veritable cornucopia of wealth — a heated home, all the furnishings, clothing, arranged language and orientation sessions, schooling for the children, job offers, gifts, money — and weeping quiet tears of grief brought on by the aching pit of homesickness.

The House

Canadians may meet refugees from the relatively wealthy, urban élite, who will fit quite easily into our pattern of urban, suburban, or small-town living; that is, the pattern of the one-family dwellings. The majority of Lao, however, are accustomed to having a fairly large number of people living in relatively small quarters. To have individual sleeping-rooms for each person is unusual. Most Lao houses have few rooms and little furniture. The climate is warm. The houses are small and simple. Much of daily life happens on the "veranda," which is about half the area of a house.

As it is for the majority of mankind, who also live in rural villages, visiting is important. During the day, when you may be carrying rice home from the mill, you stop by to visit, for it may well be hot too. A few minutes after you arrive, someone will bring you out a glass of light tea. The tea is made from a nearby plant — perhaps the leaf, or bark, or branch, or root; whichever tea it is, it is good for digestion — for the visiting too.

Meals, visiting, and visitors' sleeping all usually take place on the veranda. A simple mattress or a straw mat is unrolled,

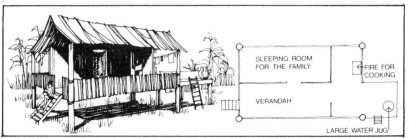

pillows and blankets are brought out, and all is well for the night. In the morning these are put away, and throughout the working day, all activity in the house takes place here and in the cooking area.

Throughout all of Southeast Asia, people are very concerned with cleanliness, and Laos is no exception. As most villages are built along a river bank, it is easy to wash — "take a bath" — in the morning and evening in the river. Clothes are also washed often, daily whenever possible. Where people do not live along running water, they haul water up out of a well and use that for bathing. The way of bathing is to spoon the water over oneself with a small dipper, soap up, then rinse off. This is more like a shower than a bath. Whatever bathing facilities sponsoring groups can make available to a refugee family will be of great importance as its members go through the many adjustments from Lao to Canadian culture.

"Come and Take Rice"

If you happen to enter a Lao house at a time of eating, you will hear the greeting: "Come and take rice." Unless you really have just eaten, you do sit down at the circle around the meal and join in.

For all Southeast Asians, the basic staple food is rice. This means that, by volume, rice is the major food in the daily diet. It is eaten for breakfast, lunch, and supper. This is very different from having a little pile of rice among a lot of other foods in the usual way Canadians eat rice. For Asians, rice is the meal, and the other foods are more like additions to the rice. In fact, in Lao, the word for *eat*, when translated literally, is to "take in rice."

There are many kinds of rice, just as there are many kinds of bread. Whereas most Southeast Asians eat white rice, the kind of rice grown and eaten by people of Lao origin is glutinous rice. White rice is usually cooked by boiling (two parts water to one part rice), but glutinous rice must be steamed.[2]

---

2.   It is a little harder in Canada to find glutinous or sticky rice than white rice, but it is carried by food stores in the Chinatown sections of larger urban centres. (Try asking for "sweet rice.") If the sponsoring group does not have access to a Chinatown, white rice is quite acceptable. It is preferable to obtain rice in fairly large quantities, ten or twenty kilo bags, for example. Convenience, precooked rice, like "instant rice" or the highly processed, boxed kinds of rice, should be avoided if at all possible. Apart from being expensive, these rices are really tasteless and also have the food value processed out of them.

Along with rice, Lao people may eat either fresh or saltwater fish, poultry, beef (either cow or water buffalo), and pork. Most people, including those in the towns, have gardens during the dry season (January to May) in which they grow spring onions, garlic, cabbages, various kinds of lettuce, green beans, peas, tomatoes, hot peppers (chili), cauliflowers, and cucumbers. Root vegetables, like potatoes, do not generally grow well in most parts of Laos but are not unknown.

Most people will have fruit-bearing trees or plants around their houses, with the common ones being banana (there are many varieties of bananas and so many ways that they may be eaten), coconut, mango, papaya, orange, and lemon (lemons are used often in cooking much as we might use vinegar). Many people also find ways of growing other kinds of foods, including pineapple, cantaloupe, watermelon, and sweet corn.

While this may, at first glance, appear to represent a rich and varied diet, the opposite is the case. For most people, the daily diet is very simple and fairly montonous: rice with a little flavouring of *pa dek* (pronounced pa-deck) and perhaps a few vegetable greens. Pa dek is a very strong-tasting, pungent paste made by salting a variety of small fish caught in the rice padis, or larger river fish, and letting this mixture ferment and age in earthen jars for several months. Meat is rarely eaten, as it is a scarce commodity, and even chicken is usually kept for special occasions.

On every kind of rating, Laos ranks as one of the poorest countries in the world, and this fact is reflected in the simple, unsophisticated Lao cuisine.

Buddhism — The Gentle Way

There are several main streams of Buddhist thought, each one tending to predominate in a particular geographic region. The form of Buddhism practised in Laos is Theravada Buddhism, and it is shared with Cambodia, Thailand, Burma, and Sri Lanka (Ceylon). The language of the Buddha was Pali, and Pali is therefore the language of the Buddhist scriptures, as well as one of the well-springs of the Lao language itself.

Although the various interpretations of the vision of the Buddha differ quite significantly, the differences are not the source of exclusivity or aggression. Nor is there a missionary or evangelistic emphasis in Theravada Buddhism, no command to go out and teach the world. For in Buddhism, the varieties of religious experience are many; the paths to enlightenment are unnumbered. The Western religious traditions are more aggressive, with the believer tending to view the non-believer (the rest of the world) with suspicion and distrust. On the other hand, Buddhism is fundamentally pacific, emphasizing tolerance and complete respect for the destiny of fellow creatures. Each one of us is on a personal path towards our eventual destiny, and that path is unique. It is therefore not the affair of other individuals to try to interfere in the life-destiny of another.

This attitude of tolerance to others is a basic component of Lao life. Acceptance of the way another person lives does not necessarily imply either approval or disapproval; it is simply a recognition of that person as he is.

Bouns — Festivals — and the Baci

As mentioned earlier, the seasons in Laos are determined by the monsoons — those winds that either carry the rains or clear the sky of clouds during the dry season. The seasons are as markedly different as winter and summer. The rains usually begin sometime in May and June and, through the next few months, increase in frequency until they start to diminish in November and December. The rice-growing season takes place during the rainy season.

In late December, the dry, cool season begins, and through the next few months there may be only an occasional rainfall. By the end of February, the land is dry and dusty. The weather begins to get warmer, and the rain still does not fall. By April, it is very hot and very dry. The time to plant the rice nursery beds is drawing near, and people begin looking for the rain.

This is the time for the first boun of the year to be held. Boun Bang Fii (pronounced "boon bung fie") — the Rocket Festival. Each village has its own Boun Bang Fii, and preparations for the boun begin some time before. In each household, the families get together, with the women and girls cleaning and decorating the house and preparing the food. The men talk together and fix the location for firing the rockets — usually in or near the wat, or along the river bank. Many people go to the wat and attend the prayer sessions with the monks.

The men start to make the rockets. These are creations of considerable skill made from bamboo, with gunpowder as the rocket fuel. The head of the rocket is usually decorated, often with sexual symbols.

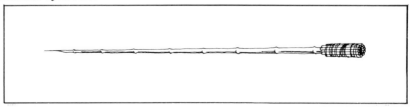

On the day of the boun, the rockets are carried in procession through the village by their creators. Each group of rocket bearers includes someone playing the *khene* (rhymes with "hen"), a wind instrument made from small bamboo tubes and a gourd, with a hauntingly beautiful, sweet, minor-key sound. Others carry the drum, or perhaps pots or kettles or sticks, to beat the rhythm of the songs being sung to the khene. They all dance through the village, singing of their rockets, of the beauty of the girls of the village, and of their own sexual prowess.

They visit all the houses, where they are welcomed with food and *lao*, a distilled and very powerful rice wine. Between the hosts and visitors, there is a continuous stream of banter and joking, which usually culminates in the girls smearing the faces and bodies of the men with pot black.

The climax of the day is the launching of the rockets, one by one. Each builder carries his rocket up the ladder and gets it ready to be fired. The fuse is lit; the rocket takes off. If it has been well built, it will soar far up into the sky and trace a graceful curve back down to the ground. A good launching is an auspicious omen, for the sky will be pierced and the rain will come to water the dry land. The cycle of rebirth begins again.

The next boun, which follows soon after Boun Bang Fii, is Pii Mei (pronounced "pea my"). This is the Lao New Year. Foreigners sometimes call it the water-throwing festival, and it is probably one of the happiest bouns anywhere in the world.

Like New Year celebrations in most cultures, it is a time to finish with the past, and all the infirmities of the previous year, and to begin afresh with the new year. It is a time of spring cleaning, so the houses are turned inside out, dusted off, washed out, and polished up. It is a time to take all the *pra* (the images of the Buddha) to the wat, where they will stay through the night of the old-new year and will be washed in blessed water by all who come through the wat. It is a time to prepare food, for it is a time when everyone visits everybody else.

During the three days of the boun itself, everywhere you go you will be splashed with water. To splash water on others is to bless them, for you are washing away the old; to be splashed is to be blessed, so you always respond with a *khop-chye* ("thank you"). Even the monks and the old people do not escape the water. It is fun, refreshing, and a thoroughly joyous boun.

Any description of Laos would be incomplete without mention of a ceremony unique to the Lao — the *baci* (pronounced "baa see"). The baci, perhaps more than anything else, is the distillation of the essential elements of Lao culture. In the baci are embodied all the special ingredients of the Lao attitude to other people.

A baci may be given to anyone: to a newborn baby and its mother, to newly-weds, to someone who is entering the monkhood, to someone who is sick, to someone going on a long trip or journey, to someone who has returned after a long absence, to a visitor in your house, to the bereaved, to anyone at any kind of boun, to someone with whom you have made a reconciliation, to one who has survived some kind of danger, or in simple thanks.

A baci may be elaborate — and it usually is at a wedding or Pii Mei — or it may be very simple. It is always a moving experience.

The central element of the baci is one person offering a blessing to another. While he does so, he ties a cotton string on the wrist of the recipient; this represents the bond between the two people and acts as a talisman against evil or harm.

For the more ceremonial baci, a kind of large conical tree (called "phaa baci") is prepared. It is made from dozens of carefully rolled banana leaves, woven together with flowers and candles, and long slender bamboo branches from which hang the cotton strings. It is placed in the centre of the room and surrounded by sweet cakes and other delicacies.

On one side of the room sit the older people and the *ma phon*, an elder who will chant the main blessing. Opposite him, on the other side of the phaa baci, sits the person for whom the baci is being held. All around the room sits everybody else — all who can crowd in.

The ma phon begins. The chant is a haunting sing-song, often in Pali, painting a poetic picture of the occasion and weaving a word-spell of grace and beauty. When he chants in Lao, he extols the virtues of the person being honoured, describes the desire of all who are present that he be protected from all harm, that he be favoured with the knowledge and wisdom to live in the way of peace and respect for others, that he be bestowed with the good regard of those who know him, and that he be the recipient of luck and good fortune. When he finishes his general chant, he gives a particular blessing to the recipient; while doing so, he ties a string first on one wrist, then on the other.

One by one, all the other people in the room do the same. Meanwhile, everyone begins "giving baci" to everyone else. While the string is being tied on one wrist, morsels of food or small glasses of lao are pressed into the other hand; these must be eaten or drunk right away. So while the baci may be moving, it is by no means a solemn event. In fact, if at any time it seems to be getting a bit stodgy, someone, often one of the old women, will call out a comment that lightens the atmosphere of the occasion.

So the baci is really a reflection of the people themselves. While life has its serious moments, and may even be harsh and demanding, laughter, joy in beauty, and a full appreciation of life's pleasures make the Lao a buoyant and optimistic people.

For the Prince will eventually recover again.

Many Girls' Names are Flowers (A Modern Lao Legend)

Young Mr. Thao and a couple of his friends were clearing a new strip of land — tangled secondary jungle growth that had never been cultivated. Using *phaa* ("machette") they cut down all the thick undergrowth, leaving a few large trees and several beautiful clumps of bamboo. The slash was burned, and the land was bulldozed. Large stumps, tangled clods of bamboo roots, stones, clumps of clay — the clearing and cleaning of all that lay ahead.

Now Thao spent several evenings working on a small plot of the land, near where the gate to the property was later located.

"What have you planted there?"

"Flowers."

"Ah ha! For someone special?"

"Well, um . . . well, I love flowers. Flowers are beautiful. And girls come to visit gardens with flowers." (That, in fact, is true.)

"So when girls come to my flowers, I have a chance to relax for a while and have some fun with them. We can joke and tease each other. Then if I'm lucky, they'll come back with their friends." He laughed. "That is really fun. Talking, joking — flirting — with girls. That makes the rest of this easier."

And it was so.

A Note on Pronunciation

The word Laos rhymes with "house," not "chaos"; the people are the Lao (rhymes with "how").

Written Lao, like English, is a phonetic script; that is, letters represent sounds. (Chinese, on the other hand, is ideographic; that is, the characters are pictures.) However, Lao, unlike English, is phonetically very precise. Each letter represents a specific sound, and no other. It is hard to use imprecise English letters (roman script) to represent precise Lao sounds, particularly with those Lao sounds that do not exist in English.

Two Lao sounds must be mentioned in particular. They are shown in roman script as "p" and "th".

In English, "ph" is sounded as "f." Thus, "fone" is written as "phone." In Lao, however, the "ph" is pronounced like a "p" followed by an "h" — something like the sound of the last two letters in "snipe." Try saying, "snipe hone"; then drop the "sni" and say ". . .pe hone." Say it again, a little faster: ". . .pe hone." Now you are saying "phone" (not "fone"!) Thus, "ma phon" (see the section about the baci) is not "ma fawn," and phon rhymes with "upon," not "home."

The "th" sounds in English are quite special and exist only in one or two other of the thousands of languages in the world. They do not exist in Lao, for example, but Lao does have a sound like "t" followed by "h". Thus, Thailand, for example, is pronounced much more like "tie land" than "thy land" or "thigh land."

Refugees landing in Malaysia from sinking ship.

4

The Chinese in Indochina

by
W.E. Willmott

History of Chinese Influence in Southeast Asia

Although Southeast Asia has been in continuous contact with both China and India for thousands of years, its early kingdoms adopted Indian rather than Chinese political and religious institutions because the Chinese traditions were not exportable. The Indian religions — Hinduism and Buddhism — provided ritual for all classes as well as theological justifications for the aspiring kings in Southeast Asia. In contrast, the Confucian political order rested on bureaucratic administration rather than military power, and its religious aspects were relatively unimportant and certainly not for popular consumption. Of all the Southeast Asian countries, only Vietnam developed in the Confucian rather than the Hindu mould, and that because it was an integral part of the Chinese empire during a thousand years, 111 B.C. - A.D. 939.

Because Southeast Asian countries were not Chinese in their institutions, Chinese migrants were culturally distinct from the indigenous populations wherever they went. Even in Vietnam, language, dress, eating habits, and the preponderance of Buddhism made the Chinese immigrants distinct. (The Chinese were more often Taoists or Confucianists than Buddhists.) This cultural distinctiveness has been both a cause and an effect of the social separation between Chinese communities and the host societies. Consequently, both social and cultural factors have been used by social scientists in defining who is Chinese in the region. Legal definitions are not particularly useful because the majority of the Chinese became citizens of the countries where they settled, and many of their children were born there. Chinese customs and organizations are therefore the defining characteristics, which indicates how fuzzy the boundaries of the Chinese communities can be. In the Muslim countries (Indonesia, Malaysia, Southern Philippines), the distinction between those who eat pork and those who do not was rather clear-cut. However, in host countries where assimilation was not difficult (Burma, Thailand, Kampuchea, Vietnam, Laos), many citizens were more or less Chinese depending on the social circumstances, and many more became less and less Chinese as the years went by.

Because of this fuzziness, the figures represented in table 1 should be read with scepticism. They are my estimates from the various statistics available (themselves sparse) on the numbers of Chinese in the various countries of Southeast Asia.

Altogether, the 15 million Chinese represent only 4.5 percent of the population in Southeast Asia, and they might be ignored by scholars and planners alike were it not for their prominent position in the economy of the region, which is out of all proportion to their demographic numbers.

These communities in Southeast Asia grew more rapidly during the colonial period (1800 - 1945) and after the Second World War, when these countries were struggling for their independence

TABLE 1

The Chinese Population in Southeast Asia

Country	Ethnic Chinese	Percentage of Total Population	
		1979	*1965*
Vietnam	1,000,000	2.0	3.1
Kampuchea	. . .	. . .	6.8
Laos	. . .	. . .	1.8
Thailand	3,800,000	8.5	8.5
Burma	500,000	1.6	1.6
Malaysia	3,730,000	28.8	34.5
Singapore	1,824,000	78.1	74.9
Brunei	47,000	24.5	26.3
Indonesia	3,600,000	2.6	2.6
Philippines	400,000	0.9	1.4
Refugee camps	100,000	78.0	. . .
Total for Southeast Asia	15,000,000	4.5	5.0

and China was undergoing a social revolution. Chinese came to the Nanyang (the Chinese term for Southeast Asia, meaning "south sea") in order to make money that they could take or send back to China. This original motivation took many of them into trade, where initially they met with little competition for the indigenous population was engaged primarily in agriculture and the small upper classes derived their wealth from tribute rather than commerce. As time passed, settled Chinese invested in manufacturing various goods, but the majority have remained in commerce, even after they have ceased to think of themselves as sojourners.

The Economic and Political Power of the Chinese in Southeast Asia

The colonial economic systems reinforced the Chinese middleman position, for few European firms were competent to trade directly with the producers. The trade between manufactured goods and local agricultural produce was therefore almost entirely in Chinese hands, with the exception of competition from the Indians in Burma, Vietnamese in northern Vietnam, and *mestizos* in the Philippines (people of mixed Spanish and indigenous parenthood).

In Indochina (Kampuchea, Laos, and Vietnam), the basis of Chinese trade was rice, spices, retailing, and import-export. A few Chinese went into agriculture, but usually into cash crops such as vegetables or pepper (in southern Kampuchea). Only in northern Vietnam, along the border with China, were there Chinese rice farmers.

In Kampuchea, the Chinese were heavily concentrated in the trading professions, both urban and rural. Table 2 presents their occupational distribution in 1962-63, when I did research in Phnom Penh. The table shows that the vast majority of Chinese were in commerce of one sort or another, and it also demonstrates that very few Khmer (the dominant ethnic group comprising 86 percent of Kampucheans) were in commerce. At that time, eight of the ten big import-export companies were Chinese, and some 95 percent of the internal trade was in Chinese hands. Furthermore, 99 percent of the 3,500 privately owned industrial firms were Chinese, representing about 90 percent of total private capital investment. The situation was somewhat different in Vietnam where there was a much smaller proportion of Chinese in the rural areas, and where some Vietnamese were in commerce. Nevertheless, the large Chinese trading firms in Saigon dominated rice export, small-goods import, and most of the small-scale manufacturing.

This is not to say that all Chinese were wealthy businessmen — far from it. As table 2 shows, a portion of the Chinese population was working class, and even among those in trade the vast majority were poor, perhaps owning no more than a portable stall and a few dry goods to sell in an open market. Nevertheless, even these small businessmen had a commercial mentality that differed markedly from the peasant culture of the majority of the indigenous population.

While the Chinese dominated most of the internal commercial economy and some foreign trade as well, their position in the political arena was far from powerful. During the colonial era, they were excluded from power by the European colonial regimes which defined them as immigrants, however long they had lived in the country. When these countries became independent, it was the non-Chinese majority that achieved power and have held it since. (Singapore is the notable exception, of course, since its population has been predominantly Chinese from its inception.) In Kampuchea, however, where assimilation has blurred ethnic distinctions, many politicians had Chinese ancestry and living connections with the Chinese community, but the tragic events in Kampuchea over the past ten years have all but eliminated the Chinese from that country.

The Chinese have thus been in a paradoxical position in Southeast Asia, enjoying considerable economic power as a community (though usually not as individuals, since most were in small-scale businesses) yet excluded from real political power. Relations between Chinese and other ethnic groups have sometimes been cordial, but there have also been moments when tempers have boiled. One such exception was the slaughter of scores of thousands of Chinese in Indonesia during the tragic events of October, 1965, when Sukarno's government was overthrown by a military coup that produced widespread disruption and violence throughout Java (see Wurfel, chapter 6). Another was the riot in Kuala Lumpur, Malaysia, in May, 1969, when Chinese lives were lost and the entire community was under fearful attack (see Wurfel, chapter 6). Most recently, the Chinese in Vietnam

TABLE 2

Economic Classes among the Chinese in Cambodia, 1962-63

Economic Class	Chinese Number	Chinese Percentage	All Cambodia Number	All Cambodia Percentage	Chinese as Percentage of Total
Peasants and Fishermen			4,950,000	86.0	*31.0*
Working:	*64,000*	*15.5*	*209,000*	*4.0*	*31.0*
Industrial	24,000	5.0	54,000	1.0	44.0
Commercial	30,000	7.0	42,000	1.0	71.0
Rural	2,000	0.5	102,000	2.0	2.0
Service*	8,000	3.0	11,000	. . .	73.0
Commercial:	*359,000*	*84.0*	*379,000*	*6.5*	*95.0*
Rural	173,000	41.0	183,000	3.0	95.0
Urban	186,000	43.0	196,000	3.5	95.0
Professional and Government	*2,000*	*0.5*	*202,000*	*3.5*	*1.0*
Total	*425,000*	*100.0*	*5,740,000*	*100.0*	*7.4*

*Includes restaurant workers.

have been persecuted since 1978, at a time of dire economic and social difficulties, natural disasters, and international strife.

Structure of Chinese Communities

One of the reasons why the Chinese remained ethnically distinct in Southeast Asian countries was the presence of a network of Chinese organizations that structured their communities. These communities did not look in the least like the peasant villages in southeastern China whence the Chinese came, for the nature of migration precluded that. Their original villages were organized on the basis of kinship, but when they migrated they left their kinship groups behind, and so various kinds of voluntary associations took their place. The Chinese in Southeast Asia (as in Canada and other countries) built associations on the basis of common locality, with members recruited from among those who came from a single county, district, or prefecture. Other associations grouped those with a common surname, such as Lee, Wong, or Lim. Still others were fraternal associations that required an oath of allegiance from their members and kept their ritual and membership secret; these were the "secret societies," some of them with origins in China, which served to protect their members from the predatory behaviour of other ethnic groups or other Chinese associations. Still other associations were built around common interests, such as trade unions, chambers of commerce, and music societies.

The memberships of these different kinds of organizations could overlap: Mr. Lee and Mr. Lim could both join the same locality association if they both came from Toysan County; two Mr. Lees could be in the same clan association but different locality associations if they came from different counties; both Mr. Lee and Mr. Lim could join the same fraternal society. Leaders tended to be officers in more than one association, and a powerful leadership network thus developed in each Chinese community that served as a quasi-government, making rules, settling disputes, and protecting the Chinese from the excesses of colonial exploitation or repression. In most colonies, the colonial administrators found it convenient to deal with this Chinese "government," and so allowed the Chinese leaders a measure of independence to administer their own communities. The French, Dutch, and Spanish formalized this relationship into systems of indirect rule, while the British permitted a more informal *modus gubernandi* to evolve.

Thus far, I have spoken of the Chinese as if they were a homogeneous group in each country, but in fact they comprised a number of different ethnic groups. At least five Chinese languages are represented in various proportions: Hokkien (the language of Amoy and its environs) is spoken by the largest number, about a quarter of all Chinese in Southeast Asia; Teochiu (from Swatow) by slightly less; Cantonese by a fifth; Hakka and Hainanese by still smaller proportions. In Indochina, the Teochiu-speaking Chinese are most numerous, especially in Kampuchea, while in Vietnam the Cantonese predominate.

It can be seen from table 2 that the Chinese in Kampuchea are found in a number of social classes. The organizations I have described above, however, recruit across class lines, with the exception of trade unions and chambers of commerce. Consequently, these organizations can mitigate class conflict as well as ethnic and personal conflicts.

From the outside, this Chinese community structure can look like an anti-governmental conspiracy of major proportions when antagonisms develop between ethnic groups. This has led some to suggest that the Chinese represent a "fifth column" for the People's Republic of China in Southeast Asia. In order to examine this question, it is necessary first to look at the policy of the Chinese government towards the Chinese residents of Southeast Asia.

The Policy of the Chinese Government

Chinese governmental policy towards emigrés has changed several times during this century. The Manchu Imperial government was opposed to emigration during the nineteenth century and, therefore, refused to offer any protection to those who chose to leave China. In 1909, however, it promulgated a citizenship law that defined as Chinese subjects "every legal or extra-legal child of a Chinese father *or* mother regardless of birthplace." This broad approach to citizenship was inherited by the Republican government after the 1911 revolution, and the Kuomintang government in Taiwan has never repudiated it, still assuming that it can speak for, and demand allegiance from, all "Chinese" anywhere in the world, regardless of their citizenship.

When the Communists first gained power in 1949, they accepted the traditional view that all Chinese were their concern, and official statements in the early 1950s stressed concern for overseas brothers and determination to support them in the face of discrimination. In 1954-55 their attitude changed towards the newly independent governments in Southeast Asia, and this necessitated a change in policy towards overseas Chinese as well. Since then, Peking has distinguished clearly between "overseas Chinese," meaning Chinese citizens resident abroad, and those citizens of other countries who are of Chinese origin. Their overall policies relate only to the former, and top Chinese leaders have encouraged the latter to be good citizens of their adopted countries.

Paradoxically, Peking alienated the overseas Chinese during the period 1949-54 by the land-reform measures that expropriated many of their families in China. Since 1955, however, Peking has solicited their support, especially since the end of the Cultural Revolution, and now they are encouraged to visit China, invest there, or even settle if they wish to. It thus allows them to express their support for the new emergent China without placing them in the embarrassing position of disloyalty to the governments of their countries of residence. Only when Sino-Vietnamese relations deteriorated towards open conflict did this policy fail.

The Chinese who live abroad are rather different from the citizens of the People's Republic of China. While feeling pride in that country's achievements, they are not necessarily in favour of its socialist programs. The older generation of businessmen, in particular, can be quite anti-Communist at the same time as they are pro-China. On the other hand, the younger generation, having become citizens of adopted countries, many of them by birth, may enter into the political life of that country with a rather radical viewpoint based on their pro-Chinese sentiments. In Indonesia, for instance, many young and locally born Chinese were members or supporters of the Indonesian Communist party. Similarly, in Vietnam, while some Chinese businessmen with Kuomintang affiliation opposed the Communist-led struggle for independence, a few joined the Viet Minh and fought as Vietnamese of Chinese ancestry for the independence of their country. Most were neutral, however. As long as China and Vietnam were friendly neighbours, they felt no ambivalence and faced no ambiguity in doing this.

Vietnam's Ethnic Chinese Refugees

Having surveyed the situation regarding the Chinese in Southeast Asia in general, we can now focus more specifically on the two countries that are providing refugees at the present time, a large proportion of whom are of Chinese origin.

The refugees from Vietnam have usually been thought of as "boat people," but in fact many left Vietnam by crossing the Chinese border. As one might expect, almost all of these were ethnic Chinese; although many have lived in Vietnam for generations. Chinese accounts provide interviews with one young man whose family had lived in Vietnam for seven generations and with an old man whose wife was Vietnamese and so he had to leave her and his children when he was forced out of the country. There are some 250,000 of these refugees-by-land, most of them from North Vietnam where the Chinese had assimilated far more than in the South. They were fishermen, peasants, carpenters, teachers, and workers, and most probably would have preferred to remain in Vietnam, since they had made their homes there for years or even decades. They have been resettled in Guangxi and Guangdong provinces, some in and around Guangzhou, the largest city in southern China. A few have made their way through China to Hong Kong, and some of these are keen to migrate to the United States, Canada, or other industrial countries. They say that they suffered increasing discrimination and prejudice and eventually were asked to leave.

The boat people have a different story. While a few of them (about 40,000 of those who got to Hong Kong) are from North Vietnam, the vast majority came from the southern part, where the socialist revolution has made far less progress and where economic problems are more severe. These were urban Chinese, and most of them were in commerce; consequently, many of them benefited from the American presence in Saigon when commerce boomed with American aid and American soldiers had money to spend. It is not surprising that the Vietnamese patriots who fought thirty years in the jungles for independence of their country should feel little sympathy with these people.

Their situation did not become desperate, however, for at least a year after Saigon changed to Ho Chi Minh City. Ultimately, three interacting forces forced them to flee. One of these factors was economic hardship, caused by a combination of the worst natural disasters Vietnam had experienced in a hundred years (droughts and floods) plus the refusal of the United States to provide the reconstruction aid it had promised in the peace agreement. In clause 21 of the Geneva Agreement, America promised to pay $7 billion towards the reconstruction of Indochina, $3.7 billion of which was to come to Vietnam to help overcome the destruction by defoliants, block-buster bombs, and napalm that had rained down on the countryside of Vietnam for so many years. Without this aid, Vietnam was faced with the prospect of her city populations starving when the floods and droughts hit agricultural areas. The government was therefore forced to move urban people into the countryside, but many Chinese did not wish to become peasants.

The second factor was the socialist transformation of the Vietnamese economy, which began in 1977 and 1978, and which accelerated because of the economic crisis. The Vietnamese Communists suddenly nationalized commerce in March of 1978, thus expropriating many Chinese businessmen in Ho Chi Minh City. At the same time, the program called for the development of socialist agriculture in newly developed regions of the countryside, and many Chinese were among the 1.5 million who went to these "new economic zones," where conditions were spartan, work was hard, and food was scarce.

The third factor was the deterioration of relations between Vietnam and Kampuchea. Had this not occurred, we might well have seen far fewer taking the desperate step of leaving everything and embarking on the South China Sea in little boats to confront pirates, wind, and rain rather than remain where they were. Because China supported Kampuchea in the conflict, the Chinese in Vietnam were seen as a potential "fifth column," and when relationships deteriorated to open warfare, the Vietnamese took stringent measures against their resident Chinese, removing them from jobs they had held for some time, denying their children schooling, and even removing their ration cards. In the face of such blatant discrimination, many chose to leave. This occurred in both North and South Vietnam.

Kampuchea's Ethnic Chinese Refugees

The situation in Kampuchea was altogether different, and there is no proof that the Chinese suffered as an ethnic group per se, although there is, of course, that possibility in a nationalistic revolution. Rather, they suffered along with all the other urban and non-peasant portion of the population. When the forces led by Pol Pot took Phnom Penh in April, 1975, the city was faced with a crisis far more immediate than that in Vietnam. For eighteen months the Americans had been bombing the countryside heavily and indiscriminately, so that half the peasant population had become refugees in the cities to escape the senseless bombs. Phnom Penh had grown from a city of half a million (when I was there in 1963) to over three million, most of them squatters living in squalor and entirely supported by American handouts of food brought into the country by American aid. Consequently, when American aid suddenly stopped, the city had less than ten days' supply of food and the danger of epidemic was extreme. Furthermore, the rainy season was only two months away, and if the fields were not prepared in time for the planting, the country would have faced starvation for another year at least.

In the face of such desperate conditions, the Pol Pot regime had no alternative but to move the urban population to the countryside as rapidly as possible to find food and to do the agricultural work necessary in preparation for the rains. Being inexperienced in mass politics (they had only been going for five years by then), they made serious mistakes, using force at times when persuasion might have sufficed, and many people therefore suffered or died in the evacuation. The figures have been grossly exaggerated by propagandists, however, and there have even been cases of falsified photographs to discredit the Pol Pot government. Unfortunately, most of our information about that period comes from refugees or Vietnamese sources.

Once in the countryside, the population was faced with difficult circumstances of food shortages, hard physical labour, and a program of socialist transformation that seemed far too accelerated to receive popular approval. Losing support, the regime became ever more repressive rather than modifying its program. Without evidence, it is difficult to say whether or not they had the choice of slowing down, but we do know that agricultural production improved, that Kampuchea succeeded in feeding the population without imports from 1976 through 1978, and that great improvements were made in irrigation and water control during that time. A trickle of refugees crossed the Thai border throughout the period 1975-78, but the flood began after the Vietnamese invaded Kampuchea in December, 1978, and established its client government in Phnom Penh in January, 1979. This invasion disrupted agriculture completely, an entire year's planting was prevented, and suddenly the Kampucheans were faced with imminent starvation. Both the invasion and starvation caused people to leave, fleeing westward into Thailand, since Vietnam was on the east.

The refugees left Kampuchea in three waves. First came those who entered Thailand during 1975-78, fleeing from the Khmer Rouge. They included many Chinese, since many would have opposed the new Communist government; some actually fled eastward, ending up in Vietnam, where they suffered the same discrimination that other Chinese now suffer there. The second wave of refugees from Kampuchea were fleeing from the Vietnamese invaders in the first half of 1979. This group included very few Chinese. The third and final wave contained those who were simply leaving because they were starving to death. Among these would be the same proportion of Chinese as in the general Kampuchean population, since starvation does not discriminate.

Among the Indochinese refugees as a whole, it is possible to distinguish a number of different categories, and the types and proportion of Chinese vary among them. Those who went by land to China were almost all Cantonese, and most of them have stayed in China. Those who escaped by boat from southern Vietnam are also primarily Cantonese, although a little under half of them are Vietnamese and a few speak other Chinese languages (Teochiu, Hakka, Hokkien, Hainam). Among the refugees from Kampuchea who fled to Thailand, there are quite a few Chinese, most of them Teochiu-speakers. Many of these latter will be able to speak Cantonese as well, however, since Cantonese was the language of commerce among all the Chinese groups in Kampuchea.[1]

---

1.   For suggested reading, see bibliography.

Part Two

Lands and Politics

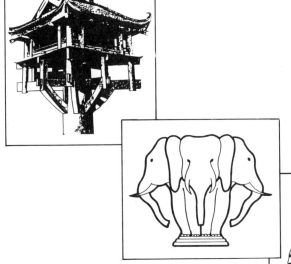

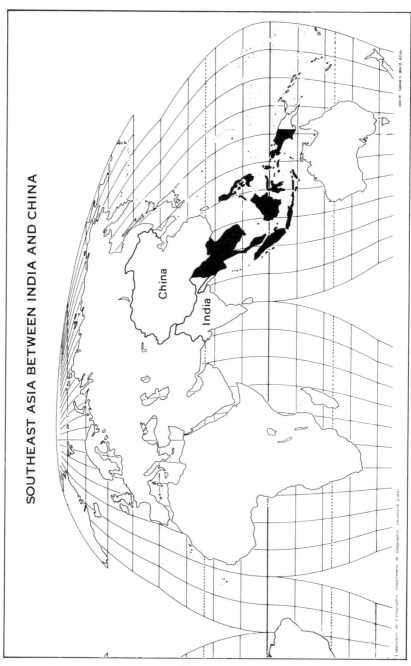

SOUTHEAST ASIA BETWEEN INDIA AND CHINA

China

India

Source: Goode's World Atlas

Laboratoire de Cartographie, Département de Géographie, Université Laval

Map 1

5

The Tropical, Agricultural Corner of Asia: An Introduction to Southeast Asia

by
Rodolphe De Koninck

The refugees of Kampuchea, Laos, and Vietnam that have chosen Canada as their country of adoption come from regions where geography plays a particularly important role in the economic, political, and cultural life of society. The link between man on one hand and land and water on the other is much stronger and more intimate than in societies such as that of southern Canada. The rupturing of this link, and the uprooting from the natural and traditional environment, is one of the more painful aspects of the tragic experience that lies behind the word *refugee*. The present chapter presents a few of the fundamental traits of the physical and human environment pertaining to the peoples of Southeast Asia.

The Corner of Asia

Southeast Asia, called the "corner of Asia" by Paul Mus, has both its own specific features and features stemming from its continental links with India and China (see map 1).

The Environment

A fundamental specific feature is the tropical character of the area. Entirely situated within the tropics, Southeast Asia is hot and wet. However, climatic conditions are not uniform, being influenced by two factors: the maritime nature of much of the area, and the extremely fragmented topography. A simple glance at a map of the region reveals the extent of fragmentation, on both the horizontal and vertical scales.

It will be seen that the area is made up of a series of more or less parallel peninsulas, and that its maritime domain is extended through a large network of islands. These narrow peninsulas and scattered islands, small and large, are studded with mountains. As a result, Southeast Asia is a veritable layered jigsaw puzzle with seas, lowlands, and mountains — often in very narrow juxtaposition.

Another fundamental feature results from the first three, that is, the tropical, maritime, and fragmented nature of the area. This fourth feature is the great ecological diversity. While maritime influences in all areas of the world tend to create a certain uniformity, in Southeast Asia the shape of the area, the origin and path of the prevailing winds and their seasonal variations (northeasterly and southwesterly) — in short the monsoon climates — have diverse effects on the different layers of the puzzle; that is particularly evident according to altitude and the axis of exposure to the west, east, northwest, and so forth.

This results in an infinite number of environments, making Southeast Asia by far the most diversified area in the world in biogeographical terms. No other territory of similar size in the world has such a diversity in the spatial distribution of temperature and rainfall levels, of plant and animal species.

It is an essential fact that Southeast Asia is a humid tropical area, dominated, therefore, by abundant rainfall and generally high temperatures and humidity. Of even greater importance, however, is the fact the tropical character contains a wide variety of climatic conditions. Thus, for example, average as well as extreme temperatures vary greatly between the low-lying and the upland areas. Within Vietnam temperatures can read well over forty degrees in Celsius in coastal towns in June, while they may drop close to freezing point in January in the inhabited hills close to the Chinese border. Contrasts are also strong between cities such as Ho Chi Minh City, where temperatures rarely drop below twenty-five degrees Celsius, and Hanoi, where warm clothes are needed during the winter months. This general variation in the climate is all the more important in view of the fact that Southeast Asia remains one of the great lumbering and agricultural areas of the world. At a more localized level, the variation is equally important and is reflected throughout the area by the contrasts between coastal and inland, elevated and low-lying zones, between land and water. The repercussions from climate are one of the major features of the economic and cultural history of the area.

The Agriculture

What are commonly called features of civilization are linked to, and may occasionally stem from, ecological characteristics. Thus, the importance of Southeast Asia as an innovative centre first appeared in the domestication of plants and in agriculture. For example, the area was one of the main homelands of rice cultivation, in particular underwater rice cultivation. Moreover, the history of Southeast Asian agriculture is an important chapter in the history of humanity. Its vitality is linked to the exceptional dynamism of the ecological conditions, where the juxtaposition of "mountains, foothills, irrigated valleys and sea coasts constituted an ideal setting for domestication."[1] Even today, Southeast Asia is one of the world centres of two great types of food-producing and agriculture — cultivation of burnt-over forest land (also called slash-and-burn cultivation) and rice growing in flooded fields.

Among the numerous reasons that explain the prevailing importance of rice, a few can be listed here.

1. It produces more food per acre than any other crop that can be grown in the tropical climate; in fact, under optimal conditions, an acre of irrigated rice yields at least ten times more calories than an equivalent acre devoted to livestock rearing anywhere in the world.

2. Rice is able to adapt itself to many environments, from regularly flooded fields to dry upland slopes.

3. In the much preferred irrigated fields, rice can be grown for centuries without much fertilizer and without any significant decrease in the yield.

4. Fish farming is easily combined with irrigated rice, the fish being reared in the ponds, irrigation canals, and flooded fields themselves. Therein lies the major protein source for the local population, which, in addition, produces a wide array of fruits, vegetables, and small farm animals on house plots.

---

1. Jacques Barrau, "L'Asie du Sud-Est, berceau cultural," *Études Rurales*, nos. 53-56 (1974), pp. 17-40.

External Influences

While Southeast Asia has been the centre of various innovations in the development of its agriculture and the set of cultural traits that are associated with it, the area also benefited from various external contributions. This is largely a result of its position at the end corner of Asia, between the Indian and Chinese spheres of influence; hence, on one of the great avenues of world geography and history. There, too, the particular configuration and fragmentation of the area have been factors; influences, techniques, peoples passing through or seeking refuge took root here and there — on an island, a riverbank, a coastal plain, a valley, a mountainside.

This great openness of Southeast Asia has made it a region of the world where particularly remarkable agricultural and cultural symbioses have been achieved. This is precisely the case for the technology and cultural ecology of wet-rice cultivation. Thus, the techniques used for controlling the water may be of local, Indian, Chinese, or European origin.

However, to this position and configuration there are numerous disadvantages as well as advantages. Southeast Asia has been not only an area of cultural exchange and activity, but also a much sought-after prize. During the colonial period, basically from the seventeenth century on, Southeast Asia has been subject to ever more perfected control and exploitation in which the tapping of resources — such as tin, timber, and, particularly, plantation crops — has played a predominant role. In fact, colonial policy brought about or often emphasized regional specialization. For example, regions such as the southern part of Vietnam (Cochinchina) were primarily devoted to the extensive cultivation of export crops (rice and rubber), while in other regions, such as the northern part of Vietnam (Tonkin), much emphasis was put on intensive rice cultivation, with relatively developed industrial activities being encouraged in the cities. The highly differential population densities that resulted from such policies, along with the establishment of arbitrary colonial borders, brought international and regional problems that are still of great consequence today.

Characteristics of the Continental Realm

The Case of Indochina

It is important to remember that the area as a whole shares the attributes of tropicality, position as a land corner and/or maritime crossroads, topographical fragmentation, and ecological diversity. However, there are differences in the intensity of these factors on many planes, principally between the so-called continental zone and the peninsular and island zone, that is, between the Indochinese and Malay realms. By its general configuration, the continental zone is relatively more homogeneous, less fragmented. Moreover, its temperatures are on the whole lower, its rainfall lighter. Finally, and especially, the geography of the area is dominated by the presence of great rivers: the Irrawaddy, the Salween, the Menam (Chao Phraya), the Mekong, and the Red. The central basin and delta of the Irrawaddy are at the heart of the geography and economy of Burma. The Chao Phraya performs a similar role in Thailand. As for the Mekong, it is the central artery of the countries of East Indochina (also called simply Indochina), that is, the three contiguous countries of Laos, Cambodia, and Vietnam; the latter is also watered by the Red River (see map 2). The plains and deltas of these rivers as well as the narrow network of coastal plains in Vietnam represent the principal, though not the sole, inhabited zones. They are also the site of the principal, agricultural production, including rice, the product par excellence of the alluvial lands of tropical Asia.

Agriculture and the distribution of those who carry it on are truly at the centre of the "Indochinese question."

The Distribution of Population in East Indochina

In the three countries of East Indochina, as in Southeast Asia as a whole, two elements of this distribution are particularly relevant: density and ethnicity.

Generally, there is a strict correlation between high population density and types of relief. Thus, while practically all the alluvial lowlands sustain high population density, often surpassing 200 inhabitants per square kilometre, the more elevated zones have a very low density, often below 10 inhabitants per square kilometre. Vietnam offers probably the most striking example of this contrast. There, the delta, coastal, and alluvial zones, particularly the Red River delta (Tonkin Delta) with 20

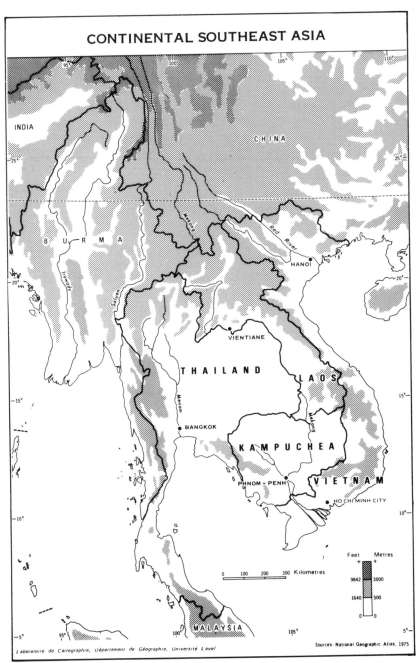

CONTINENTAL SOUTHEAST ASIA

INDIA

CHINA

B U R M A

HANOI

Red River

Mekong

Salween

Irrawaddy

VIENTIANE

THAILAND

LAOS

Menam

Mekong

BANGKOK

KAMPUCHEA

VIETNAM

PHNOM - PENH

HO CHI MINH CITY

MALAYSIA

Feet	Metres
+	+
9842	3000
1640	500
0	0

0   100   200   300   Kilometres

Sources: National Geographic Atlas, 1975

Laboratoire de Cartographie, Département de Géographie, Université Laval

Map 2

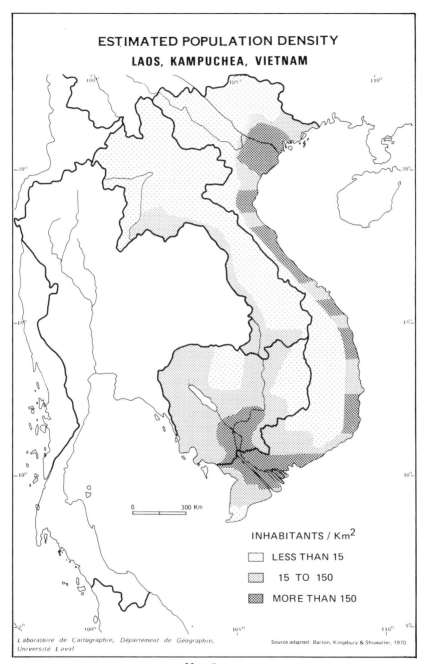

ESTIMATED POPULATION DENSITY
LAOS, KAMPUCHEA, VIETNAM

0   300 Km

INHABITANTS / Km²

LESS THAN 15

15 TO 150

MORE THAN 150

Laboratoire de Cartographie. Département de Géographie. Université Laval

Source adapted: Barton, Kingsbury & Showalter, 1970.

Map 3

percent of the country's area, hold 85 percent of the population. In some of the rural districts of the Red River delta, the average population densities surpass 450 persons per square kilometre, which, by the way, is ten times higher than the rural population density in the Niagara peninsula in southern Ontario. Finally, in the lowlands themselves, there is an even more pronounced concentration in the flood plains of the great rivers. In this regard, the central plain of Cambodia is an excellent example.

There is really nothing unusual about this relationship between population and geography, especially since the main crop of the area is rice grown in flooded fields. However, this pattern is of particular importance, given the superimposed ethnic distribution. There exists a close relationship, overall, between four components: natural environment, dominant type of agriculture, ethnic group, and population density. Here again a fundamental opposition can be discerned. This opposition is seen, on the one hand, in the great river valleys of the continental zone, located on a north-south axis and heavily populated by a dominant ethnic group basically engaged in irrigated rice cultivation; and, on the other hand, in the more elevated zones, largely still covered with forests and sparsely populated by a large number of ethnic groups engaged in a much less productive form of agriculture — essentially cultivation of burnt-over forest land, which has a low yield per acre and is unable to sustain a high population density.

It is important to mention, if only briefly, the genesis of ethnic localizations. It is generally recognized that Southeast Asia, including the continental part, was populated over thousands of years by a succession of great waves of migration from the north, principally during the second millenium B.C. The majority of these migrants came down into the area through the great river valleys, which cut through the mountainous zones and link the lowlands of Indochina to the heart of Asia. However, these were not the first inhabitants. They were preceded by peoples whose origin is much more obscure and who were largely driven back into the less hospitable, less fertile elevated areas. Today, the descendants of these indigenous peoples are very few. What should be emphasized is the process of successive waves of migration, whereby the previous inhabitants were driven towards the interior, the newcomers seizing the coasts and river valleys as they advanced.

In fact, this process had important variants. Land migrations from the mountainous zones of South China took place until after the beginning of the historical period. Later migrants thus came up against consolidated populations whose agriculture was relatively sophisticated, and therefore they settled in the mountainous zones that were not completely occupied by the peoples previously driven there. The resulting "ethnic distribution" is quite complex, especially in the countries of the continental zone.

Today, there still exists a fundamental distinction between the dominant peoples occupying the great river basins and the coastal and alluvial plains and those who have taken refuge in the mountain and forest regions. The first group includes the Burmese, the Thai, the Khmers, the Lao, and the Annamese (Vietnamese); to the second belong such peoples as the Karens and the Chins in Burma, the Miao in East Indochina, and even more ancient occupants, such as the Hmong of the Annamite chain of mountains, called specifically, the "Montagnards."

During recent times, particularly the nineteenth and twentieth centuries, the ethnic mosaic has undergone a series of additional alterations, with the Chinese and Indian migrations being facilitated and encouraged by the development of colonialism. These migrants came by sea, swelled the population of cities, and basically helped supply the labour force for mining and plantations. Despite its importance, this accelerated process of labour migrations by Indians and especially Chinese was simply parallel to the previously described process, which involved essentially the occupation of the various mountainous areas of the region. To understand this issue, it is important to consider the agricultural stakes.

The Importance of Agriculture

More than half of East Indochina is rough terrain unsuited for intensive agriculture. Nor are all the plains suitable; a large proportion of their soil is lateritic (hard and infertile) and hence unsuitable for cultivation. These are not the only reasons for the relatively slight proportion of land surface devoted to agriculture; there are many others, such as climatic conditions, common types of agriculture, the vicissitudes of history and of wars, and ethnic antagonisms. Be that as it may, the problem is serious: a total of less than 15 percent of land surface is devoted to agriculture.

In each of the countries of East Indochina, around 75 percent of the working population is engaged in agriculture. The most important crop, by virtue of land surface and work force, is

TABLE 1

National Space and Agriculture

Principle Source: ATLASECO, 1979.

	Vietnam	Laos	Cambodia
Estimated population 1980, in millions	50.8	3.7	5.0
Area in square kilometres	329,556	236,800	181,035
Density (inhabitants per square kilometres)	154	16	28
Percentage of labour force in agriculture	73	75	75
Percentage of land surface under cultivation	17	4	17
Percentage of agricultural area in rice	86	71	?
Agricultural density (inhabitants per square kilometre under cultivation)	907	39	162

irrigated rice. In Vietnam and Laos, the agricultural scene is dominated by rice. While, according to the above figure, rice might seem to occupy a less important place in Cambodia, the whole contemporary economic history of that country has been dominated by that very cereal. Rice growing is the principal activity, the principal skill, the life-blood of the entire area; hence, the question of the availability of land is also vital.

In this respect it is important to emphasize the fundamental distinction between the technology of agriculture on burnt-over forest land, whether used to produce rice or other food, and irrigated rice cultivation. The former is based on shifting cultivation, and therefore reforestation is possible and there is little or no ploughing of land or need for road and irrigation. The latter involves total occupation of the soil, which must be deeply plowed and requires hydraulic engineering. Although these two types of agriculture do not necessarily require the same soils, they often compete, and the latter type is always victorious.

This explanation was needed to evoke one of the consequences of the necessary expansion of the land area devoted to agriculture, particularly in Vietnam where there is great pressure on territorial resources; that is, the increased pressure on the ecological domain of the refugee peoples of the interior, generally engaged in relatively extensive agriculture (see table 1). This helps us to understand the conflicts between upland and lowland peoples such as the Hmong and the Lao. It is equally obvious that there is a serious imbalance in agricultural density between Vietnam on the one hand and Laos and Cambodia on the other. The existence of this imbalance, which, as we have seen, is partly of colonial origin, is one of the central problems that confronts the three countries today.

The consolidation and expansion of the agricultural realm is an integral part of current development plans in the area. While they were applied in a particular way in revolutionary Cambodia, the principles governing such development were clearly recognized in Vietnam, notably in the Five-Year Plan of 1976-80. Thus, almost a third of the investment budget of the state was devoted to agriculture, and especially to the infrastructure, that is, irrigation. Investing in irrigation means repairing, maintaining, improving, expanding the hydraulic network. Expanding the hydraulic network means consolidating permanent agricultural settlements; this means moving populations. As a result, since 1975 in Vietnam, at least four million people have reportedly been moved into the "new economic zones" where many other crops besides rice can be grown. Finally, the ultimate symbol of the new forms of land occupation and utilization is the marked development of the forest industry. The exploitation of the important timber resources of Laos and Vietnam is now the object of ambitious planning. The remaining "ecological layers" are about to be integrated even more profoundly into the national economies.[2]

---

2.   For suggested reading, see bibliography.

Cambodian refugees receiving food rations at Sakaeo, Thailand.

Refugees from Vietnam arrive in Malaysia.

6

Indochina: The Historical and Political Background

by
David Wurfel

Southeast Asia, the region that has sent such a tragic flow of refugees to other parts of the world in recent years, is peopled by those who know conflict and suffering. Some countries were severely damaged by fighting in the Second World War. Then, only a short time after the surrender of the Japanese, both Indonesian and Vietnamese nationalists had to begin an armed struggle to win independence from European colonial masters — the Dutch in Indonesia and the French in Vietnam. The Philippines has experienced both peasant and ethnic rebellions in the last three decades, as has Burma. In 1965-66 hundreds of thousands of Indonesians lost their lives in the bloody retribution that followed an unsuccessful coup. But nowhere has the population suffered as much, or as long as in Vietnam and in the other two countries of what was once French Indochina, Laos and Cambodia. (In 1975 the new leadership adopted the name "Kampuchea," a transliteration of the original Khmer term for the country that the French had called "Cambodge.")

Socio-Economic Conditions

Social and economic life has, nevertheless, carried on with remarkable persistence, considering the catastrophic events that have occurred. Though the standard of living in Indochina is very modest from a Canadian perspective, there are important variations to be noted and understood. Considering the great upheavals, it is obvious that accurate statistics are not available, but some figures must be cited to allow comparison. Recent estimates put the average per capital income in Vietnam at $120 (less than that of India), whereas for Laos it is said to be only $85 and for Kampuchea, $70 — perhaps generous in 1980. This is to be compared with about $10,000 in Canada. Another measure of welfare in any society, which is usually representative of conditions generally, is infant mortality. In Vietnam in 1978 it was estimated at about 30 per 1,000 births, while in Laos and Cambodia it was about 130.

Aside from indices of physical well-being, perhaps the most important measure of the quality of a society is the literacy rate. Here the contrast is even sharper. While literacy is reported at 85 percent of the adult population in Vietnam, it is only 30 percent in Laos and somewhat higher in Cambodia. This is a reflection of the fact that formal education has long had a higher value in Vietnamese society. It is also true that Vietnam is more industrialized than its two smaller neighbours; this was true even when the French left, but government policy in North Vietnam capitalized on that advantage.

Whatever the comparisons of national averages, however, the variety of the human condition is much greater. Before 1975 there were great gaps between the rich and the poor in Laos, Cambodia, and South Vietnam — especially the latter. Most rural households probably lived on a family income no greater than the national per capita average. Though there are no reliable estimates on income distribution in these countries, observations in Southeast Asian countries where figures do exist would provide the basis for surmise that even in good times more than a third of the populations lived below the poverty level, seriously malnourished and just barely "making it." In Vientiane, Phnom Penh, and Saigon, on the other hand, there were numerous millionaires, hundreds of families that could afford to send their children to France for an education, and thousands more who enjoyed family automobiles and other modern conveniences. In North Vietnam, however, though average per capita incomes were no higher, the distribution was much more equitable so that extremes of poverty did not exist.

To compare the style of life in Indochina with ours merely in statistical terms is inadequate, to say the least. International statistical comparisons at their best cannot give weight to the satisfactions of village life, nor do they properly evaluate goods and services produced by the household for family consumption, or even measure exact equivalents. The papaya or coconut picked from a yard does not show up in the accounting. Air-conditioning is certainly not a felt need if one lives mostly on the veranda of a bamboo house, wisely slowing the pace of life when it gets too hot. Nor is an automobile of any particular advantage when both economic and cultural life is sustained within the village. And a diet that eschews the heavy reliance on red meat that we crave may make for healthier bodies.

Thus, before the devastation of war, it is fair to say that in the villages of Laos, Kampuchea, and Vietnam, most people were able to maintain a life-style that encompassed adequate nutrition, close-knit families, self-respect, and considerable joie de vivre. Village resource always seemed adequate to put on a special feast or annual festival.

In our review of the social-economic situation, we must remember that Vietnam has 44 percent of the land and about 85 percent of the population of Indochina. We recognize also that socio-economic conditions in Vietnam are more advanced than in Laos and Kampuchea. What we have not noted so far is the attitudes that go along with these measurable differences, and the cultures from which these attitudes spring.

A Major Cultural Boundary

Indochina straddles the border between two of the world's major cultural regions — and that is the origin of its name. Vietnam stands on one side, in the region heavily influenced by Chinese culture; Kampuchea and Laos stand on the other side, greatly affected by the Indian subcontinent. Vietnam is thus dominated by Mahayana, the Chinese school of Buddhism, along with other Chinese religions, while Laos and Kampuchea are even more thoroughly Buddhist, but in the Theravada tradition that originated in Sri Lanka. Writing systems, political traditions, and architecture all follow the same divide. The cultural gap between Indianized and Sinicized Southeast Asia is at least as great as that between Catholic or Protestant, Western Europe and Orthodox Eastern Europe — and in Canada many of us are aware of those differences.

This is not to suggest, however, that the countries of Indochina are mere appendages of Chinese or Indian culture. The relationship is much more subtle, and more complex, than that. In fact, Southeast Asia is itself one of the major cradles of civilization. Archaeological digs in the region date the first homo sapiens at about 40,000 years ago. A recent find in Thailand has located pottery that is about 10,000 years old, among the oldest pots discovered anywhere in the world. A site in northeast Thailand, near Laos, has revealed a bronze-using civilization dating back 5,000 years, much earlier than the appearance of bronze in ancient China, and as early as in the Near East. Thus, when Chinese and Indian influences began to penetrate Southeast Asia more than 2,000 years ago, there were already organized societies of some sophistication.

And despite the importance of the impact of these two great Asian civilizations, Southeast Asia — and thus also Indochinese — societies have retained certain common and distinct characteristics. The family system, for instance, called *bi-lateral* by anthropologists because kinship is reckoned through both the male and female lines, has given women a more prominent role than elsewhere in Asia. It has also made for a greater looseness and flexibility of social organization than in the patrilineal societies of China and India. (Chinese influence in Vietnam has mixed patrilineal with earlier bilateral kinship practices.) The earlier animist religious beliefs and practices in Southeast Asia have also survived the introduction of Buddhism. The village *dinh*, or community altar, in Vietnam is often found where no Buddhist temple exists. In Laos and Cambodia, animism was intermingled with local Buddhist belief. Chinese and Indian influences are, in fact, more noticeable at the élite than at the peasant level.

Nevertheless, this cultural gap, along with more recent political history, must be understood if we are to appreciate the depth and the motivations of the tensions and conflicts that exist in Indochina today, many of which spill over into the refugee community in Canada.

Early History

The Khmer people had organized a proud and powerful empire in the Mekong Delta (covering both present-day Kampuchea and portions of neighbouring countries) even before the Vietnamese won their independence from a thousand years of Chinese imperial control in 939 A.D. (For the Vietnamese were able to combine from an early date extensive cultural borrowing from China with a fierce anti-Chinese nationalism.) But when the Vietnamese did establish their own kingdom, organized and ruled very much in the Chinese style, they soon became the most dynamic force in the area. Population growth was relieved by a steady push of Vietnamese settlements to the south, until they began to displace the Khmer in the Mekong Delta during the seventeenth century. From then until the nineteenth century, the Vietnamese and Thai competed for the chance to either dominate or annex Khmer territory, with each being successful from time to time. The Vietnamese in the same period exercised indirect control over several of the Buddhist princes and pagan tribal chieftains who ruled in Laos. They also had to fight off Chinese efforts from time to time to reannex Vietnam. Thus, before the arrival of French colonialism, the main axes of contemporary conflict had already emerged: Vietnamese fear of Chinese dominance; Khmer and Lao distrust of the Vietnamese for the same reason; and Vietnamese feelings of cultural and political superiority over their Indianized neighbours to the west.

French Colonialism

The preponderance of the French power in Indochina was first demonstrated in 1859 with the capture of Saigon and was confirmed in 1893 when the Thai recognized French control of the three kingdoms of Laos. Vietnam, which had been a unified "empire," was divided by the French into three parts: Tonkin in the north, Annam in the centre, and Cochinchina in the south. Passports were required to move from one part to another. Only Cochinchina was directly ruled as a French colony; the other two portions of Vietnam were officially governed indirectly through local Vietnamese mandarins and the puppet emperor residing in Hué. But over time the French impact became more and more direct.

Cambodia and Laos were also ruled indirectly. In fact, there were so few Frenchmen involved in colonial administration there that the French had to rely on Vietnamese, who were the first in Indochina to be trained in French schools, to staff the lower ranks of their civil service. Thus, though the Cambodian and Lao kings had accepted French protectorates so as to forestall the encroachments of their neighbours, as "protectorates" gradually came to resemble "colonies," the Vietnamese were in positions of authority in any case. This only reinforced the historical hatred of Vietnamese by Lao and Khmer.

Just as Vietnamese were used as administrative appendages of French colonialism in Laos and Cambodia, so also did the Chinese minority in Vietnam become an economic adjunct to the colonial regime. Foreseeing economic benefit, resident Chinese actually aided the French takeover. By 1937 Chinese constituted nearly 4 percent of the population of Cochinchina, with more than 100,000 in the Saigon-Cholon area alone. The Chinese population in Tonkin and Annam was less than 1 percent. (Cambodia also had a large Chinese population: almost 3.5 percent.) But the Chinese dominance of trade and commerce made their numbers seem even greater than they were. The French, continuing the system established by indigenous monarchs, ruled the Chinese indirectly through the *chef de congrégation*. The congregation ran Chinese schools and hospitals, collected taxes, and generally maintained discipline in the Chinese community (see Willmott, chapter 4). In Vietnam, this arrangement helped to keep the Chinese a separate, self-contained group and hence complicated their problems in the post-independence era. Only in Cambodia did substantial intermarriage with the local population take place in spite of these barriers, thus speeding Chinese cutural assimilation to Khmer society.

At the same time the French were creating a plural society, their increasing exploitation of the colonial economy, and the tight control exercised over any native political expression, was helping to provoke a nationalist reaction, not of "Indochinese" nationalism — even though there was an Indochinese Communist party formed in 1930 under Ho Chi Minh — but by three distinct nationalisms for three peoples with different languages, outlooks, and political traditions. Nationalism was espoused first in Vietnam and most vigorously by the highly educated youth who were aware of developments in other parts of the world. For some Vietnamese intellectuals, the nationalism of Sun Yat Sen in China was the model, especially after he successfully overthrew the emperor in 1911, but such respect for China never eliminated the resentment against the local Chinese minority, whom Vietnamese called "Hoa."

After a series of nationalist organizations and even a few uprisings had been crushed by the French, the arrival of the Japanese in 1941 created new dangers and new opportunities.

Some nationalists chose to accept Japanese support against the French, while others decided to oppose both foreign powers. A new coalition called the Viet Minh, under the leadership of Ho Chi Minh, sought and received both Chinese and American assistance in its nationalist struggle against the Japanese, and the French who were co-operating with them. When the Japanese surrendered in August, 1945, the Viet Minh were strong enough to enter Hanoi and, on September 2, declared Vietnamese independence. Within a few weeks, by prior Allied agreement, the Chinese Nationalist Army occupied northern Vietnam in order to "receive the Japanese surrender." They "received," or even appropriated, a great deal of booty as well, reinforcing the negative side of the Vietnamese love/hate relationship with China. When the Chinese finally agreed to leave in the spring of 1946, they did so only after extracting an agreement from Paris, now determined to re-establish French colonialism, that Chinese residents would be accorded a legal status equivalent to that of French citizens.

The First Indochina War

In order to have French troops re-enter the North peaceably at the time of the Chinese withdrawal, Paris had also agreed with Ho Chi Minh to recognize his Democratic Republic of Vietnam as a "free state within the Indochinese Federation." But as soon as the French military was re-established in Hanoi, the apparent concession was forgotten. Further negotiations with Ho failed, and in December, 1946, fighting broke out between the French and the DRV (still referred to by journalists as the "Viet Minh"). The First Indochina War had begun; it lasted for eight years.

While the Viet Minh fought the French, the Lao and Cambodians, both under royal leadership, were able to negotiate their independence. But Viet Minh-supported rebel groups existed in each country as well, the Khmer Rouge (in Cambodia) and the Pathet Lao.

The Viet Minh victory at Dienbienphu finally caused the French — after eight years of an increasingly costly war — to negotiate their withdrawal from Indochina in a conference at Geneva. The Geneva Agreement of July, 1954, established the seventeenth parallel as the "cease-fire line" and allowed the Democratic Republic of Vietnam, with Ho Chi Minh as president and Hanoi as its capital, to establish control of the North formally. At about the same time, the American-backed government of the

Catholic mandarin, Ngo Dinh Diem, was created in Saigon, though it had no status under the Geneva Agreement. Cease-fires also applied in Cambodia and Laos, clearing the former of the Khmer Rouge but allowing the Pathet Lao to regroup in two northern provinces of Laos. The tripartite International Commission for Supervision and Control, which was to supervise the cease-fire, included Canada.

Soon after the cease-fire, there began the first major refugee movement of this generation: the exodus of nearly a million mostly Catholic Vietnamese from the North, led by their priests and transported by the United States Navy. (More than 50,000 on the other hand, went from South to North.) These priests believed, and were encouraged by the "Voice of America" in this thinking, that it would be impossible for a Catholic community to survive under communism. They became stalwart supporters of the Diem regime in the South, which welcomed them with open arms. (Hundreds of thousands of Catholics remained in the North, however, and continue to celebrate religious observances.)

Because Ho was regarded as the "father of his nation" while Diem had only recently returned from abroad, the Saigon president had a hard time bolstering his nationalist credentials. One method used — not unusual in the Southeast Asian context — was to crack down on the local Chinese. In 1956 they were forced to become Vietnamese citizens, while all aliens were denied business licenses in eleven occupations (for example, grocers, rice millers, petroleum dealers) known to be largely in Chinese hands. Restrictions were also placed on the operation of Chinese schools. But economic retaliation by the Chinese business community softened the implementation of the new regulations. Despite the citizenship change, the ethnic Chinese community in South Vietnam, nearly a million strong, remained spirited and relatively cohesive, losing little of its extensive economic influence. But Chinese, even if legally Vietnamese, were allowed little or no access to civil service positions. Externally, the Saigon regime painted Red China as the greatest enemy, whereas North Vietnam welcomed economic and then military assistance from Peking.

The Second Indochina War

After Diem consolidated his regime, and after it became apparent to Hanoi that the nation-wide elections provided for in the Geneva Agreement could not be held, thus preventing peaceful reunification of the country, the armed conflict resumed in 1960 between Communist-led nationalists and the pro-American, anti-Communist Vietnamese in the South. The Second Indochina War had begun; it was to decide whether Vietnam would remain divided or would be unified under Hanoi's dominance.

The cease-fire in Laos had broken down even earlier. A pro-American government could not be maintained in Vientiane without an American-backed coup. Finally, the great powers met again at Geneva and the United States agreed to a coalition government with the Pathet Lao. From 1962 to 1975, Prince Souvannaphouma was prime minister of such a coalition, but it could not prevent the re-emergence of fighting in the countryside. The American escalation in Vietnam, including intense bombing of the North, forced Communist supply lines into Laos, thus linking the fighting in the two countries.

In 1970 Cambodia, which had until then been the only peaceful oasis in Indochina under the fiery nationalist leadership of Norodom Sihanouk, became involved in the increasingly bloody conflict. Sihanouk was overthrown by a military coup in March, while he was out of the country. General Lon Nol headed the new pro-American regime. By April 30 the U.S. troops had entered Cambodian territory en masse to "find and destroy" a Communist headquarters. It is not clear whether the headquarters was ever found, but for the Khmer people a tragic new era had begun. The Vietnamese-supported Khmer Rouge quickly gained control in most rural areas, while the Lon Nol government hung on in Phnom Penh with American support. Before U.S. troops left Cambodia, South Vietnamese forces — numbering nearly 50,000 — entered; they stayed much longer. Most Cambodians regarded this as merely one more of the historic Vietnamese invasions. Saigon forces pillaged and looted and, in some instances, engaged in fire-fights with Lon Nol's forces, whom they were supposed to be "aiding." The bitterness created was often taken out on Vietnamese residents of Cambodia, thousands of whom fled to Vietnam. This was merely one more confirmation of the fact that ethnic antagonisms were stronger than political bonds.

The course of the war, with all of its internal and international ramifications, is much too complex to recite here. Americans began withdrawing after a negotiated cease-fire in 1973, but fighting continued among indigenous parties until the Communist capture of Saigon in April, 1975, and a guerrilla victory in

Cambodia at about the same time. Just prior to the American evacuation of Saigon, thousands of Vietnamese left too, with several hundred ending up in the Toronto and Montreal areas. Their departure took place in an emotionally supercharged atmosphere in which U.S. and Saigon government spokesmen promoted talk of a "bloodbath." Those who left hurriedly were mostly those with close links to the American presence in Vietnam and who had been persuaded that they would be in great danger if they remained. President Thieu flew to England. In Cambodia, on the other hand, the premier remained behind, hoping for reconciliation, so that the exodus of pro-American Khmer was not so great.

After April, 1975

As events unfolded, however, the trustfulness of Premier Long Boret was badly misplaced. There was indeed a bloodbath in the new Kampuchea. In Vietnam, however, it has not materialized. Many former officials of the Saigon regime, both military and civilian, remain in "re-education camps" to be sure, and the restriction of freedom is as great as most observers would have expected, but there have not been any mass executions.

The devastation and dislocation this war caused is for us almost unimaginable. In South Vietnam about 10 million people — mostly farmers, or more than half the total population — were uprooted primarily because of American bombing of the countryside. Every city and town was swollen to overflowing, while hundreds of new refugee camps were created. Saigon jumped from 500,000 population in the 1950s to about 3 million in the early 1970s. The collapse of farm production made the country heavily dependent on U.S. aid. When that aid ended in 1975, there were at least 3 million unemployed and severe food shortages. In North Vietnam, on the other hand, it was primarily cities that were bombed, so that rural populations were augmented by urban evacuees, and industrial production was most severely damaged. Throughout Vietnam the attempt to raise agricultural production in recent years has been handicapped by thousands of bomb fragments and countless unexploded mines and artillery shells embedded in the soil. This is not surprising if we remember that the Americans dropped 25 million bombs on Vietnam during the years — or more than it dropped during the Second World War and the Korean War combined — and more tonnage was dropped on Laos than on Vietnam! Thus, the toll of civilian war casualties (nearly 2 million Vietnamese killed and wounded by 1975) did not end when the war stopped; there are still hundreds of farmers incapacitated every year merely trying to fight the battle against hunger.

In Laos there were also hundreds of thousands of refugees from rural areas during the war. But the disruption was undoubtedly the greatest in Cambodia. There suffering was postponed until 1970 and the American and South Vietnamese invasion designed to destroy Viet Cong sanctuaries. Soon thereafter, Communist-led guerrillas seized control in much of the countryside, and widespread bombing made refugees of more than half of the population. Phnom Penh, the capital, had more than quadrupled in size from 1970 to 1975 when those guerrillas, under Pol Pot, came to power. Then Phnom Penh was forcibly evacuated — to provide manpower for rice planting, it was said — and ruthless retaliation was undertaken against those perceived to be enemies or potential enemies of the regime. The resultant death toll has been estimated at anywhere from 50,000 to more than 2 million; even the lower figure, probably closer to the truth, is not based on solid data. Should 50,000 deaths prove accurate, however, it would still constitute the heaviest toll, in percentage terms, of any revolutionary aftermath in Asia.

Most students of Indochinese affairs assumed that after 1975, with strong governments of a common ideological stripe in each of the three countries, there would be stability and order in the region. But deep-seated historical antagonisms, the prolonged economic crisis that was the aftermath of war, and the impact of world politics upset these assumptions. The only predictable trend was the discontent of middle-class elements who suffered economically and politically in the face of fundamental social change pushed by a determined leadership. From Vietnam and Laos many of these people continued to flee; Cambodia, on the other hand, was a prison from which there was no escape.

Refugees from Laos

Historical antagonisms emerged to influence events in each of the three countries. Most of the Vietnamese population of Laos, which had constituted the majority in many towns, had left in the 1940s soon after independence. But Vietnamese influence again rose substantially after 1975. The Pathet Lao had long received the guidance and support — some claimed control — of Hanoi.

When the Pathet Lao became the government, the fears of the old élite (often of royal lineage), which were based on ideological differences, were reinforced by the traditional hatred of the Vietnamese. Since Vientiane, the capital, stands just across the Mekong from Thailand, and since Thailand was familiar territory, with many family links at the élite level, escape was an understandable and relatively easy choice. The middle class included a signficant admixture of Chinese who were almost equally uncomfortable in a Vietnamese-dominated situation.

Another major component of refugees from Laos is the Hmong, whom the French called "Meo." They are one of several hill peoples who make up nearly half of the country's population. They are separated from the lowland Lao both by language and by style of life, being hunters, fishers, and shifting cultivators. The social distance between upland and lowland inhabitants of Laos has always been great. The Hmong, who in the 1960s constituted less than 10 percent of the Lao population, were recruited by the Central Intelligence Agency to organize a counter-attack on Pathet Lao forces, which were then already strong. The Hmong fought loyally for their American paymasters and against their traditional enemy, the Lao. But when the Americans left hastily and the Pathet Lao became the government, the Hmong feared vengeance, and apparently with some justification. In May, 1975, an official Pathet Lao newspaper stated that "Meo must be exterminated." Three years later, the prestigious French daily *Le Monde* reported that 10 percent of the Hmong population of about 300,000 had been killed as a result of Pathet Lao campaigns against them, about equal to the number of Hmong casualties in the fifteen years of fighting before 1975. A determination to survive has led thousands of Hmong to flee their tribal homelands — itself an extremely difficult decision — to seek refuge in Thailand. And more are coming.

Refugees from Vietnam

The eruption of ethnic conflict in Vietnam was largely a consequence of shifts in world politics. We have already pointed out that there have long been tensions between Vietnamese and resident Chinese, or Hoa. It is also true that despite the absolute necessity for North Vietnam to receive, and even solicit, help from Peking during the Vietnam War, the traditional fear of Chinese dominance — revitalized by widespread looting during the Chinese occupation of 1945-46 — caused Hanoi to resist successfully the sending of Chinese combat troops on to Vietnamese territory.

After 1975 the Sino-Soviet dispute intensified, even as U.S.-Chinese relations were rapidly warming. The Soviets offered rehabilitation aid to win Vietnamese support. The Chinese were disinclined, because of closer Soviet-Vietnamese ties, to be as generous. In fact, by mid-1978 they were sufficiently angered to cut off all aid. Furthermore, Chinese support for the newly established Pol Pot regime in Kampuchea helped bring Hanoi and Peking into direct conflict.

We now know that between 1970 and 1975 the once dominant Vietnamese influence in the Khmer Communist movement was resolutely eliminated by Pol Pot, resulting in bloody purges. Thus, in 1975 Pol Pot, allied with China and following revolutionary strategies at utter variance with Vietnam's, set out to right "old wrongs," such as the disputed border. Pol Pot revived some of Sihanouk's border claims against Ngo Dinh Diem from the early 1960s and proceeded to reinforce them with military action. These pin pricks goaded Hanoi, which presumed that the Khmer should recognize both the cultural and ideological superiority of the Vietnamese, into broader retaliation. The Vietnamese were encouraged in this course by their primary source of military supply, the USSR, which was upset by the strident anti-Soviet tone of Pol Pot pronouncements. Hanoi also calculated, with some justification, that the bloody repression of Pol Pot had made his government so unpopular that, despite traditional anti-Vietnamese animosities, they would be welcomed as "liberators." So in early December 120,000 Vietnamese troops crossed into Kampuchea. By January a pro-Vietnamese "revolutionary council" had been installed in Phnom Penh and Pol Pot forces had been dislodged from most provinces.

China, not wishing to be regarded as a "paper tiger," decided to "teach Vietnam a lesson." Peking sent 100,000 troops forty kilometres across the Vietnamese border on February 17, 1979, and destroyed two dozen towns. Less than three weeks later, however, they withdrew. Needless to say, the dramatic escalation of Sino-Vietnamese conflict affected the status of the Hoa. (It is also ironic that the United States, which had fought the Vietnam War "to prevent Chinese domination of Southeast Asia," now supported China in this dispute.)

Chinese residents of Vietnam had, in fact, been pawns in the dispute for many months before the actual outbreak of fighting. During 1978 more than 150,000 Hoa returned to China, at the invitation of the Chinese government and with the co-operation of the Vietnamese. Hanoi was anxious to remove them away from the China-Vietnam border and out of sensitive jobs, whereas Peking wanted to use their departure as a means of destabilizing the economic situation in Vietnam, and at the same time they would charge that the Hoa had been "ruthlessly expelled." After the Chinese invasion, Vietnam's policy hardened, rather understandably. Many Hoa were suspected of complicity in the Chinese attack, for they had maintained their cultural and linguistic identity whether Vietnamese citizens or not. In northern Vietnam, the Hoa were called together in neighbourhood meetings and given the choice of returning to China (or Hong Kong) with government co-operation, or moving to the "new economic zones" in the South to join with ethnic Vietnamese in the difficult but necessary task of restoring more land to agricultural production. Very few Hoa, who were almost all urban workers, professionals, and businessmen, chose the rugged life of this second option. Nor was it popular among the Chinese living in the South.

In southern Vietnam, economic policies had at least as much to do with the exodus of the Hoa as did international politics. Floods and famine helped produce hardships that encouraged ethnic Vietnamese to leave as well. Since 1975, in addition to the inability to cultivate many thousands of hectares because of the residue of American bombing and herbicides, Vietnam suffered a serious drought in 1977, followed by floods in 1978 that inundated 2.5 million acres of farm land. The shortfall in rice production was nearly a third of the annual requirement. In November, 1978, the government's rice ration for urban dwellers dropped from eleven kilograms per month to little more than half that. Because of fairly equitable distribution, there has been no reported starvation, but malnutrition became widespread. (In contrast, the rice ration provided by the United Nations High Commissioner for Refugees in his camps during 1978 was fifteen kilograms per month!) Vietnamese conditions in 1979 were apparently somewhat improved.

At the same time — unwisely according to some observers — Hanoi was pushing policies to transform southern Vietnam from a capitalist to a socialist economy. There were pragmatic bases for some policies, however. Growing evidence of hoarding and profiteering by merchants led to stringent currency reforms. In

March, 1978, the government took over most private businesses. Since trade and commerce was primarily in Chinese hands, the impact on the Hoa community was devastating. As fortunes dissolved overnight, there were suicides, attempts to circumvent the new regulations, and the realization on the part of many that the time had come to move on. At the same time, the Five-Year Plan called for the transfer of nearly two million people from overcrowded urban areas back to the countryside — to the new economic areas.

For a merchant, large or small, who had had a major portion of his savings wiped out by the currency reform, and who was to be reduced to a meagre government salary — or perhaps total loss of employment — if he did not go to the designated rural area, departure for abroad (especially when he did not have full knowledge of the magnitude of the risks) seemed like a very desirable alternative. One wealthy Chinese from the Mekong Delta told me that he had not experienced any racial discrimination before his decision to leave. "They (the government) just don't like capitalists," he said. And as bad as the treatment sometimes was, nowhere is there any evidence of massacres of the Hoa, as was the case with Indonesian Chinese in the mid-1960s.

Comparison with the Indonesian Chinese

The Indonesian situation provides us with a very useful comparison, in fact. Though there are a number of parallels in the fate of the Indonesian and Vietnamese Chinese, it is probably fair to say that the experience in Indonesia was worse, while opportunities for emigration were much less.

From September 30, 1965, Indonesia experienced an attempted coup and counter-coup in rapid succession. The upheaval led to the complete removal of President Sukarno from power within a few months and his replacement by General Suharto. Both Communists and Chinese were blamed for the unsuccessful coup of September 30, with much less evidence for the latter than the former charge. But in the context of political instability and economic hardships in 1966-67, Indonesian Chinese became scapegoats. Within weeks pro-Communist Chinese organizations were banned and Chinese universities burned. In December, 1965, a demonstration in Medan, South Sumatra, against the Chinese consulate turned violent, and demonstrators entered the Chinese quarter looting, burning, and hacking residents to death. Scores of Chinese were killed. The situation in North Sumatra was worse. Muslim mobs seized Chinese schools until they were all closed by the government. The local military ordered all Chinese evacuated from the area. In rioting which followed, hundreds of Chinese died.

In May, 1966, Peking sent boats to pick up refugees, but they were not allowed to land until September. Later that year, an East Javanese commander banned all Chinese wholesale trade. When some Chinese actually tried to resist the forcible closing of their stores, Muslim youth rioted, again burning and killing. But the worst incident was in West Borneo in 1967 where Chinese villages were attacked and burned and several hundred Chinese killed; 45,000 fled to nearby towns.

Only by 1968 did conditions begin to improve. Central government moderates finally established firm control and Muslim fervour cooled. Over 100,000 Chinese had fled Indonesia, about half to China, and the rest to relatives and friends in Hong Kong and other Southeast Asian countries. There was no refugee status for them in North America, for there had been no outcry on their behalf in the press. The United States and Canada supported the Suharto government. It was staunchly anti-Communist. The difference in our reaction to the plight of Chinese refugees then and now makes one wonder whether humanitarian or political criteria really control policy.

Recent Flows of Refugees from Indochina

In any case, many thousands of refugees have left Vietnam, both Hoa and ethnic Vietnamese. It is tragic that the Vietnamese regime has tolerated, perhaps knowingly, considerable corruption in the arrangements for refugee departure. This amounted to an informal "exit tax," which venal officials found possible because most of the refugees leaving had considerable savings. (One of the more bizarre twists in the refugee saga is that ethnic Vietnamese in 1979 offered bribes to acquire false identification cards as Hoa, because it made exodus much easier; in more normal times this would have been an unthinkable indignity for most Vietnamese.) These corrupt arrangements often involved the use of unreliable vessels, grossly overcrowded, and thus the numerous tragedies at sea.

Nevertheless, throughout 1978 and 1979, while the North American press was mounting attacks on the Vietnamese for their terrible "expulsion" of the refugees, Hanoi, in co-operation with the UN High Commissioner for Refugees was allowing orderly departure by air for both Paris and Hong Kong. And in January, 1979, months before the Geneva conference on Indochinese refugees, the Hanoi regime announced a policy of open emigration, even approving 10,000 exit visas under the new arrangement.

The flow of refugees from Kampuchea since 1978 is a reflection both of the terrible famine and of the fact that it has become easier to escape since the overthrow of Pol Pot by the Vietnamese. Men, women, and children from all walks of life have crossed the Thai border in increasing numbers. And hundreds of thousands more are still encamped along that border just inside Kampuchea.

We have tried to survey the life-styles, the historical experiences, and the economic hardships that have shaped the values and created the dreams of the peoples of Indochina, inducing many to flee their homelands. We must recognize that almost all refugees felt an acute lack of freedom under the new regimes that established themselves in 1975. In part this must be understood as the inevitable consequence of social revolution, though there were certainly many cases as well of brutal and unnecessary repression.

In any case, as we welcome the refugees who have finally arrived in Canada, we must remember that they come from a variety of social and cultural backgrounds. If we respect them as human beings, we will do our best to understand those backgrounds and appreciate the differences among them. Khmer, Lao, Hmong, Vietnamese, or Chinese are not just "Orientals." They are each a people with a rich heritage that will in time make a valuable contribution to the Canadian mosaic.[1]

---

1.   For suggested reading, see bibliography.

The Hai Hong aground off coast of Malaysia.

7

Why Can't They Stay in Southeast Asia? The Problems of Vietnam's Neighbours

by
Richard Stubbs

On June 15, 1979, the world's press reported that Vietnamese refugees landing on Malaysia's beaches would be shot. The reports were based on an announcement made by Malaysia's deputy prime minister, Dr. Mahathir. He suggested that drastic measures might have to be used to enforce Malaysia's policy of towing refugee boats back out to sea, wherever possible, after providing them with basic supplies. Amid the outcry that ensued and the rush by the Western media to cover the expected slaughter, a number of questions were raised: What makes Vietnam's neighbours so fearful of the refugees that they are forced to take such extreme actions? Why should the Vietnamese refugees not stay in Southeast Asia? Should North Americans and Europeans be sympathetic to the problems the refugees pose for these countries of first asylum? It is to these questions that the following section is addressed. Dr. Mahathir's pronouncement was as much a cry of frustration as it was a threat: he was determined to make the rest of the world aware of the enormity of the problems faced by Vietnam's neighbours. For many of the countries of first asylum, most notably Malaysia, Thailand, Hong Kong, and Indonesia, refugees had been arriving since 1975. During 1978, however, the numbers increased dramatically. For instance, by November, 1978, Pulau Bidong, the main

camp in Malaysia, which was originally built to accommodate
12,000 occupants, housed 25,000 refugees. As table 1 indicates, in
March, 1979, the exodus reached major proportions. By mid-June,
over 75,000 refugees were strewn along the east coast of peninsular
Malaysia, and there was every prospect that things would get still
worse. In the Malaysian camps, every refugee that was relocated
was replaced by three new arrivals; in Thailand the ratio was 1:10.
Just as discouraging for the governments involved were the assess-
ments of a number of competent authorities that there were
between 1 and 3 million more Vietnamese who might possibly take
to the boats.

It should also be noted that these were not the only refugees
in Southeast Asia. Hong Kong, a major destination for refugees
from the northern areas of Vietnam, was facing an increasing
number of arrivals from mainland China. During 1979, over
200,000 are estimated to have entered Hong Kong from the
Chinese province of Guangdong: 20,000 entering on "visiting" visas
and another 110,000-150,000 sneaking past the border patrols
and British security forces to live with relatives already resident in
the crown colony. The Malaysian state of Sabah has taken in over
100,000 Muslim Filipinos who have fled the war in the southern
island of Mindanao. And, of course, as 1979 wore on the stream of
Cambodian refugees entering Thailand became a flood. In fact, in
1979 Southeast Asia became the arena for a desultory game of
enforced musical chairs played by over a million people. It is not
surprising, then, that government officials from other Southeast
Asian countries, notably Thailand, Indonesia, Hong Kong, and the
Philippines, were in sympathy with Malaysia's policy. The
problems being created for the countries of first asylum were
formidable.

Racial and Social Problems

One line of thought in Europe and North America is that,
from a cultural point of view at least, the best place to resettle
the refugees is within the region. With the exception of the most
recent Khmer refugees in Thailand (see Thomson, chapter 8), this
viewpoint ignores the social problems of the area as well as the
political pressures faced by the governments of the countries of
first asylum. Of crucial concern to each government involved is the
threat that the refugees pose to the social and political stability of
the region. Because 70-80 percent of the refugees leaving Vietnam
during 1979 and 1980 are ethnic Chinese, their presence could well

TABLE 1

Malaysia's Predicament 1975-June, 1979

Year	Arrivals	Towed to Sea	Landing	Resettled in Other Countries	Number in Camps
1975	2,802	1,342	1,460	1,081	379
1976	1,732	274	1,458	356	1,481
1977	7,430	633	6,797	2,798	5,480
1978	64,328	4,959	59,309	15,956	48,893
Total to 1978	*76,292*	*7,208*	*69,084*	*20,191*	*58,893*
1979					
January	7,433	2,600	4,833	2,440	51,286
February	4,993	1,623	3,370	2,594	52,062
March	13,625	5,088	8,537	4,844	55,755
April	19,038	7,412	11,626	4,736	62,645
May	28,313	13,462	14,851	4,853	72,643
June	17,015	11,253	5,762	2,819	75,586
Total to June 21, 1979	*166,709*	*48,646*	*118,063*	*42,477*	*75,586*

Source: Malaysian government, cited in *Far Eastern Economic Review*, August 31, 1979.

intensify racial tensions that already exist between the resident overseas Chinese communities and other ethnic groups.

Malaysia is the country most preoccupied with this problem, and it was one of the chief reasons for Dr. Mahathir's dire warning. The ethnic composition of Malaysia is complex: 47 percent Malay, 34 percent Chinese, 9 percent Indian, 4 percent Dyak, 2 percent Kadazans, 3 percent Other Natives, and 1 percent Other. The main social division, however, is between the two largest ethnic groups, the Malays and the Chinese. The cultural division is further compounded by religious differences. The Malays are all Muslim and the influence of Islam on their lives is considerable. The Chinese, on the other hand, are Buddhists, Confucianists, or Taoists, or some combination of these. Each racial group has established a base within Malaysia. The Chinese community, which grew steadily throughout the nineteenth and twentieth centuries as successive waves of immigrants reached the area, has come to dominate the economic life of the country. The Malays, who are the largest ethnic group and who claim special rights as the indigenous people of the area, have protected their interests through their political power. However, both groups have sought to diversify their base of power — the Malays in the economic sphere, the Chinese in the political realm. The Chinese have acknowledged the need to allow Malays more participation in the commerce and trade of Malaysia; in turn, the Malays have traditionally governed in a coalition with parties representing the other ethnic groups. Nevertheless, the situation is precarious and there is a continuing preoccupation with "racial arithmetic" and the need to promote national unity and avoid open racial conflicts.

The fear of racial violence and the importance placed on preventing any situation that might increase racial tensions are rooted in past experiences. For the older generations of Malaysians, the racial violence that occurred directly after the surrender of the Japanese in 1945, and which pitted Malays against Chinese, was testimony to the way pent-up frustrations can quickly escalate to produce vicious racial attacks. The more recent race riots that followed the May, 1969, election remain a fresh reminder. While the clashes were confined to a few major cities, most notably to Kuala Lumpur, and the death toll was not as high as some people had feared (estimates range from 170 to 800 killed), for all Malaysians the experience was both traumatic and salutary. Certainly a widespread consensus has developed within the country that a repetition of the May, 1969, incidents should be avoided at all costs.

Hence, for a government determined to avoid any situation that might provoke racial violence, the possibility of large numbers of ethnic Chinese refugees landing on peninsular Malaysia's west coast beaches is particularly daunting. First, if the Chinese refugees are allowed to settle in Malaysia, then the racial arithmetic could be altered. This is a prospect that has aroused the more militant Malay nationalists. The Malaysian government has also to keep in mind the resurgence of the Islamic faith, which has given Malays more confidence in demanding greater recognition of the importance of Islam within Malaysia. A great influx of non-Muslims is, therefore, unthinkable; indeed, it is interesting to note that the Malaysian government is reported to have scoured refugee camps looking for Khmer Muslims that could be brought to Malaysia. Second, a more specific and immediate problem for the government is the possibility of Malay villagers who populate the east coast of the peninsula taking the law into their own hands and attacking the refugees who are often viewed as invaders. The fear is that this could spark racial confrontations throughout the country. It is not surprising, then, that the Malaysian government has watched events unfold with a good deal of trepidation, and that it has argued that there is no alternative but to take a strong stand.

Other Southeast Asian countries have similar concerns. Because of the important role they play in the economies of the region, the Chinese have frequently been mistrusted. The Philippines has placed legal restrictions aimed at the trading and financial activities of Chinese. In Indonesia some of the bloodletting that followed the unsuccessful Communist coup of 1965, and during which over 200,000 people were killed, can be attributed to anti-Chinese feelings. Even the government of Singapore, where the population is roughly 85 percent Chinese, has refused entry to refugees on the grounds that such action might antagonize their ethnic-Malay, Muslim neighbours. The racial factor has certainly played a part in the reluctance of Vietnam's neighbours to take in the fleeing refugees.

Economic Problems

Vietnam's neighbours, like Vietnam itself, are relatively poor countries. The governments of Southeast Asia just do not have the resources to resettle large numbers of refugees, and the economies of the region cannot absorb such an influx of labour. Recent figures show the annual per capita income (in U.S. dollars) of the countries of first asylum as: Indonesia, $337; Thailand, $482; Phillippines, $500; Malaysia, $1,154; Hong Kong, $2,700; and Singapore, $3,314. This should be compared with Canada's per capita income of nearly $10,000. While these figures would indicate that both Hong Kong and Singapore might be capable of taking in quite a few refugees, it must be kept in mind that Singapore's over 2 million population is already crowded into 580 square kilometres, and that Hong Kong is in a similar situation with more than 5 million people spread over only 1,040 square kilometres. With in excess of 4,000 people per kilometre in each country, both governments are reluctant to put even greater strains on their space by allowing thousands more to try to find places to live. Hong Kong has done as much as is possible, but the problems are becoming enormous. Singapore has refused entry to practically all refugees.

The economic pressures on the governments of the region to refuse entry to refugees are considerable. Let us, again, take Malaysia as an example. Malaysia is currently nearing the end of the period covered by the Third Malaysia Plan (1976-80), under which the government publicly committed itself to reducing the proportion of Malaysia's households below the poverty line from the 1975 level of 44 percent to 34 percent by 1980. In particular, the intention is to reduce poverty among Malaysia's agriculture-based households from 63 percent to 49 percent, for it is in the rural areas that Malay poverty, which is of greatest concern to the Malay-dominated government, is most evident. The Malaysian government is also committed to enhancing the role of Malays in the economy in general, thereby reducing the gap between the average monthly income of Chinese families (Malaysian $245.00 in 1976) and Malay families (Malaysian $100.20 in 1976). Politically, then, it is very difficult for the Malaysian government to redirect funds out of current programs to help resettle refugees. Funds are scarce and the uproar that would accompany such a move would be disastrous for a government whose major aim is stability and unity. Also, of course, such an influx of labour would be very difficult to absorb. Unemployment and especially under-employment are major problems for all Southeast Asian governments. The economies of these countries just cannot cope with the influx of such numbers of people. This gives rise to the argument put forward by the countries of first asylum that the economic capacity for absorbing the refugees, and not geographic proximity, should be the criterion for deciding where the refugees will end up.

One additional point should be noted. The very presence of such large numbers of refugees has had a detrimental effect on the economies of the areas involved. Black markets have thrived along the Thai-Kampuchean border and to a lesser extent along the east coast of peninsular Malaysia. Inflation has also been a problem as the scarce resources of food and medical supplies have been sought after by ever-increasing numbers of refugees. In many instances, the local population suffers considerably. To make things worse, a great deal of resentment has arisen over the differential treatment accorded the refugees and the local population. Why, ask local peasant farmers, should we have to work for our living when the refugees receive aid (through the United Nations) for just sitting around? When this problem is allied to racial distrust, the possibilities for social unrest are evident. This leads us directly to the problems posed by the camps themselves.

The Camps

An important ingredient in the reluctance of Vietnam's neighbours to accept the refugees is the experience of other governments that have allowed temporary camps to be established on their territory. As in the case of the Palestinian refugees, these "temporary camps" have too often become permanent. The governments of Malaysia, Thailand, Hong Kong, and Indonesia have all expressed the fear that once the furore over refugees dies down in Europe and North America, the allocation of refugees will slow down. Moreover, with the countries of the industrialized world having creamed off the skilled, educated, and physically fit, the countries of first asylum will be left with the diseased, the aged, the illiterate, the unskilled, and those without relatives in the industrialized world — not a pretty prospect. Tan Sri Ghazali Shafi, the home affairs minister of Malaysia, harked upon this theme when he suggested that Vietnam should set up United Nations-run camps on its own soil. Others have suggested that the Americans might like to establish some large camps on their territory — in Guam, for instance. Both Vietnam and the United States have declined to take up these suggestions. Similarly, Australia and France have said they will not allow camps to be established on their territory — Australia along the northern coast and France in New Caledonia. These actions do not encourage the countries of Southeast Asia to open their doors.

For Thailand, the camps along its border with Kampuchea present a special problem. Prior to mid-1979, the Thai government was very reluctant to accept any refugees from either Vietnam or, more importantly, Kampuchea. However, in June, 1979, Thai patrols forcibly repatriated about 42,000 Cambodians across a heavily mined wasteland. The horrors of this experience and the resulting world-wide publicity, plus the provision of some inducements by the Americans — including the delivery of fifteen M-48 tanks and the promise of some F-5E aircraft — was enough to change Thai policy. But now the Thai government must face the possibility that the camps will become a target for advancing Vietnamese troops and that Thailand will thus become embroiled in the Kampuchean War.

The Importance of the Region

Why should we, the citizens of the industrialized countries of North America and Europe, consider the problems of Southeast Asia as important to us? Apart from the obvious humanitarian considerations, which surely few can ignore, there are a number of strong arguments that demonstrate that our interests are closely tied to the political, social, and economic stability of Southeast Asia. First, Southeast Asian countries produce a large number of commodities, some of which are crucial to the economies of the industrialized world. Apart from significant amounts of timber, palm oil, and spices, the region produces over 80 percent of the world's natural rubber and about 50 percent of the world's tin. Also, Indonesia and Malaysia are exporting increasing amounts of petroleum, particularly to Japan. Any major social disturbance in the countries of first asylum could seriously jeopardize the continued supply of these commodities and create great difficulties for specific industries in North America and Europe. Of similar importance to many trading countries is the security of the Straits of Malacca, one of the busiest sea lanes in the world. No Western government would like to see one of the countries bounding the straits involved in racial and political strife.

Second, it is important to the industrialized countries of the West to ensure the integrity and political stability of the governments and countries that have traditionally been their friends and allies. In this regard, Lee Kuan-Yew, the prime minister of Singapore, has argued that the exodus of refugees from Vietnam and Kampuchea is a plot on the part of Vietnam's Communist government to create chaos in the countries of first asylum and thus allow the indigenous Communist organizations in these countries to subvert the governments. While the motives of the Vietnamese may be much less Machiavellian and much more tied to domestic factors than Lee suggests, nevertheless, the consequences of the flight of so many refugees may be such that the political, social, and economic problems that ensue will indeed provide fertile grounds for the expansion of Communist influence. Hence the cost to the Western world of resettling the refugees and thus alleviating some of the pressures of the countries of first asylum should be considered a necessary investment in order to limit the erosion of Western power.

It is certainly in the interest of the West to seek to minimize the ill effects of the movement of so many refugees. If, as has been argued, our economic and political interests can best be served by maintaining the social stability of Southeast Asia, then the resettling of refugees in Western industrialized countries can be defended as both a very practical and a most humane policy.

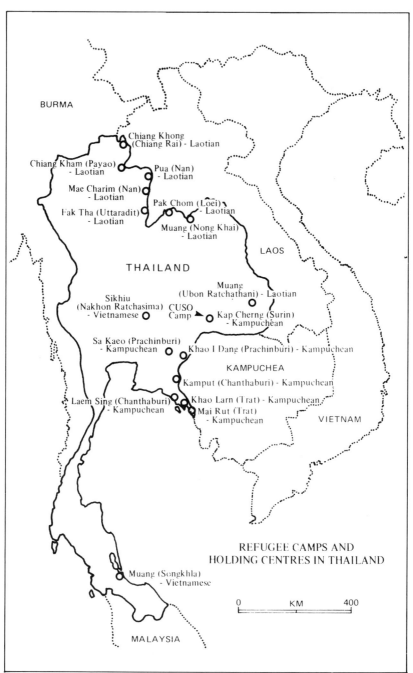

BURMA

Chiang Khong
(Chiang Rai) - Laotian

Chiang Kham (Payao)
- Laotian

Pua (Nan)
- Laotian

Mae Charim (Nan)
- Laotian

Pak Chom (Loei)
- Laotian

Fak Tha (Uttaradit)
- Laotian

Muang (Nong Khai)
- Laotian

LAOS

THAILAND

Muang
(Ubon Ratchathani) - Laotian

Sikhiu
(Nakhon Ratchasima)
- Vietnamese

CUSO
Camp

Kap Cherng (Surin)
- Kampuchean

Sa Kaeo (Prachinburi)
- Kampuchean

Khao I Dang (Prachinburi) - Kampuchean

KAMPUCHEA

Kamput (Chanthaburi) - Kampuchean

Laem Sing (Chanthaburi)
- Kampuchean

Khao Larn (Trat) - Kampuchean

Mai Rut (Trat)
- Kampuchean

VIETNAM

REFUGEE CAMPS AND
HOLDING CENTRES IN THAILAND

Muang (Songkhla)
- Vietnamese

0   KM   400

MALAYSIA

Source: Map of Thailand Showing Refugee Camps and Holding Centres. CBERS, Bangkok.

8

Refugees in Thailand: Relief, Development, and Integration

by
Suteera Thomson

About 400,000 refugees have entered Thailand during the past thirty-five years. The first wave, from 1950-59, consisted of three groups: Chinese who were remnants of the Kuomintang army of Chiang Kai-Shek (1950); Vietnamese who fled following the Viet Minh 1954 victory at Dienbienphu; and Burmese who left Burma after General Ne Win's takeover in 1959. According to the 1976-77 census figures, of the estimated 75,000-90,000 who came in during the first wave, about 65,000 remain.

A much larger second wave of about 166,000 refugees entered Thailand between April, 1975, and September, 1979. Almost all of them came by land, and most of them came from Laos. A much smaller number came by boat from Vietnam. About 500 illegal immigrants came during this period from Cambodia and Laos.

A third wave consisted entirely of Cambodians, who started to move into Thailand during October, 1979. Most of these refugees were placed in the holding centres at Khao I Dang or at Sa Kaew.

Characteristics and Motives of Recent Indochinese Refugees

According to one study, of the Indochinese refugees arriving in Thailand between April, 1975, and September, 1979, only 10 percent indicated a desire to return home. Most of the refugees opted to go to third countries, while a small number wanted to stay in Thailand.

Dr. Pornchai Busayakul of Mahidol University's Faculty of Social Science reported at a symposium on refugees at Chantaburi, Thailand, in December, 1979, that the majority of Laotians (61 percent) and Vietnamese (72 percent) had received five years or more of formal education. Forty-three percent of the Laotians had been civil servants, and 51 percent of the Vietnamese had professional skills. These characteristics and the desire of these people to find new homelands are reflected in the following statistics: by May, 1979, 90,000 of these refugees had left for twenty-one third countries. The United States, France, and Australia had accepted 45,000, 34,000, and 6,000 respectively; of the 1,200 who came to Canada, 600 are Vietnamese, 200 Laotians, and about 400 Cambodians.

The 145,000 displaced Cambodians, entering Thailand from October, 1979, reflect a different background and motivation. Over 80 percent of the 112,000 Cambodians now at Khao I Dang have indicated a desire to return to their homeland; only 12 percent of Cambodian-Chinese with formal education and professional or trade skills would prefer a third country; and 5 percent with Thai family ties would prefer settlement in Thailand. (It must be remembered here that many of the middle-class intellectuals had been killed by Pol Pot.)

The majority of the displaced Cambodians in Thailand, therefore, are not good candidates for third country settlement. It remains to be determined how long, and under what conditions, they could continue to live in Thailand. How best can they be helped and prepared for their future resettlement in their homeland, Cambodia? The remainder of the chapter will examine these questions.

Thailand, A Country of Asylum

After the Vietnamese captured Phnom Penh in January, 1979, large numbers of Cambodians began to congregate along the Thai border. Many spilled over the largely unmarked dividing line between the two countries. At first the Thai government refused to become involved. In June of that year, the Thai government moved at least 45,000 of these displaced Cambodians back across the border. This process resulted in the deaths of consider-

TABLE 1

Refugee Population in Thailand*

Refugees (1950-59) **	*64,893*
Chinese refugees	11,270
Vietnamese refugees	40,318***
Burmese refugees	13,305
Indochinese refugees	*166,025*
(April, 1975 - September, 1976)	
Land refugees	
Laotians	140,909
Cambodians	16,650
Vietnamese	1,590
Illegal immigrants	
Laotians	120
Cambodians	433
Boat people	
Vietnamese	5,770
Displaced Cambodians	*145,389*
(October, 1979 - February, 1980)	
Khao I Dang	112,151
Sa Kaew	24,487
Kamput	2,670
Mairoot	6,081

*Thai Ministry of Interior
**These figures are based on the 1976-77 census.
***More than 60,000 Vietnamese refugees came to Thailand in 1954. About half of the refugees were sent back to Vietnam via the International Red Cross in the 1960s.

able numbers of the Cambodians. International pressure was brought to bear on the Thai government. Finally, in October, 1979, the Kriangsak government announced an "open door" policy for displaced Cambodians. The Thai government gave an "illegal alien" status to these Cambodians. The Sa Kaew Holding Centre, fifty kilometres from the border, was opened shortly afterwards for displaced Cambodians, the majority of whom were sick and suffering from hunger and malnutrition. This was followed by the opening of the Khao I Dang Holding Centre, eight kilometres from the border. The Thai government asked the United Nations

High Commissioner for Refugees (UNHCR) to co-ordinate all foreign assistance contributions, and the International Red Cross together with the Thai Red Cross to co-ordinate all medical assistance. There are now more than thirty foreign relief agencies assisting UNHCR in camp operations. Thai military personnel from the Supreme Command are in charge of the camp's security.

How long can the Thai government continue to implement its present humanitarian policy? Some difficult issues remain to be resolved. When the Cambodian conflict erupted along the Thai border, about 80,000 Thai peasants, living close to that border, were evacuated to safer ground. A large number of these affected Thais still await a proper resettlement program. These people and other Thai villagers living nearby observed trucks loaded with food, water, and firewood going into the newly constructed camps for Cambodians. They observed large numbers of foreign personnel, including medical doctors, working in the camps and living in the best housing quarters. These local Thais, unable to get into camps, were also open to rumours and misinformation concerning what seemed to them like high standards of living enjoyed by displaced Cambodians.

Such problems caused the Thai government to insist recently that all foreign assistance be carefully recorded and that policies be followed that ensure equitable treatment of refugees and local Thais living in the vicinity of the camps.

How much assistance has actually been provided? Since 1975, the cost of supporting the large infux of refugees to Thailand has been borne by the UNHCR, foreign governments, the Thai government, and private groups. The UNHCR provided $33 million up to August, 1979. This money was for food, shelter, health care and sanitation, water, electricity, and transportation. Substantial contributions in the form of basic commodities, such as rice, powdered milk, and cooking oil, were also received from foreign governments. Private groups provided small quantities of basic necessities as well. The Thai government has provided $25 million for camp personnel and administration, land, and materials.

The Thai public, lacking adequate information or contact with the refugees, has become extremely skeptical. For several years Thais have heard about widespread killing in Cambodia carried out by Pol Pot and the Khmer Rouge. This was followed by the Vietnamese invasion and the establishment of the Heng Samrin regime in Phnom Penh. So the Thais are afraid that the large influx of refugees from Cambodia could become a Trojan horse inside their country. They are also concerned that Thai support of refugees could indirectly help the Khmer Rouge, thus prolonging the war in Cambodia.

In addition, despite the influx of considerable foreign exchange, many Thais fear an adverse effect upon their economy resulting from the refugee problem. To date, local producers have not generally benefited from these outside funds. Finally, they are aware that the cream of the refugees — the better skilled and better educated — are the first to go to third countries; the rest remain in Thailand.

From Relief to Development

Three stages in the life situation facing all refugees can be identified. The first is the relief, or emergency, stage, in which survival is the objective and the attainment of food, clothing, medical care, and shelter represent the means. Those who have visited the refugee camp at Khao I Dang or Sa Kaew agree that the refugees' conditions have improved greatly in the past six months. The basic needs have been taken care of to some extent; the relief stage is over.

The second stage is a developmental one involving the attainment of self-reliance and the active participation of all refugees in their new communities. This stage consists of opportunities for training, involving new income-generating and social skills, and increasing interaction with people in the larger community. It entails increasing mastery by the refugees over the forces that have governed and contained their lives. Obviously, this is a difficult stage to complete, one not easily attained or even entered into by many refugees. Nevertheless, it is essential for the successful movement from development to the final stage of integration.

The last stage either sees the refugee become a permanent member of his adopted society or sees him return to his homeland better equipped to help in the rebuilding process required there. Again, not all refugees reach this third stage.

One of the main problems is that there is little organizational help in the developmental stage. Relief agencies usually focus on the first stage of the process and are neither oriented towards nor equipped to foster development. Also, most development agencies have been reluctant to become involved with refugees. This is usually because they lack the training and orientation, or resources, for the emergency stage of the process.

However, one such agency that has been involved with refugees in the past is the Canadian University Service Overseas (CUSO). So it was possible for CUSO field workers in Asia to view the problems of Indochinese refugees from both a short-term (relief) and longer-term (development) perspective. CUSO envisaged refugee camps in which management and decision making increasingly were shared between Thai organizations and the Cambodian refugees themselves. (At present, foreign personnel dominate the decision making of the UNHCR.) CUSO's perception of development stresses the utilization of local resources and increasing the involvement of local people in decisions affecting their lives; in short, self-reliance. From this orientation emerged a proposal, accepted by Thai and UN authorities, for a management organization, the Thai Task Force for Displaced Cambodians, which was to be applied to a new camp at Karb Cherng Surin, involving 10,000 refugees.

The uniqueness of the program is the emphasis on active participation of the refugees in camp activities. Two Thai universities and twelve Thai non-government organizations (NGOs) are involved in the planning and operation of the camp's activities. Cambodians, eventually, will participate in the planning and decision making. Four thousand children under seventeen will be provided with preschool, primary, and secondary education in the Khmer language. Two thousand adults will be involved in training in such areas as health care, sanitation, and nutrition and in various aspects of community development, including agriculture and skill development of different types. These trainees will be able to provide services to other refugees in the camp in the area of their specialty. Talented refugees will be sought in order to involve them as trainers. Thais will be used as trainers only when necessary. After the first six months (beginning June, 1980), the refugees should be able to rely increasingly upon themselves. This will lessen the need for financial and other outside assistance. The cost of all operational services for this six-month period is estimated to be thirty-eight cents per person per day.

Similar programs of training and services will be provided for the Thais in the vicinity of the camp. Food and other supplies will be purchased directly from the producers. A Thai non-governmental organization is already actively involved in the process. One way it is assisting is by making it possible for food to be purchased directly from the primary producers. By eliminating the middleman, the producers will receive several times more for their products than is usually the case. Moreover, the UN agency will pay a good deal less for these agricultural products than when having to purchase them through the middleman.

These commercial benefits obtained by large numbers of local Thai farmers will help to narrow the gap between their standard of living and that enjoyed by the Cambodian refugees. If this process develops as it is intended to do, and if the military conflict in adjacent Cambodia subsides, the people of the northeast can hope for improved relations between Thais and Cambodians. And from this experience in northeast Thailand, perhaps, can be found more lasting solutions to the plight of refugees in other parts of the world.

Part Three

Problems of Resettlement

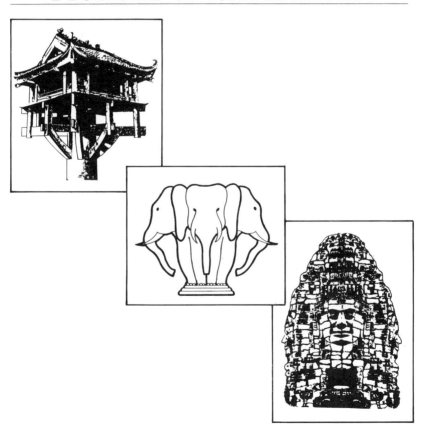

Vietnamese family arriving in Montreal.

9

Canadian Policy on Indochinese Refugees

by
Howard Adelman,
Charles Le Blanc,
and Jean-Philippe Thérien

Introduction

This chapter describes the genesis of Canadian legislation and policy on the recent migration of Indochinese refugees. As part of the background, Canadian policy towards other refugee groups arriving in Canada since 1945 is also sketched. The core of the chapter is a study of government decision making rooted in recent changes in Canadian immigration law.

International diplomatic efforts dovetailed with decisions on the resettlement of Indochinese refugees and were reinforced by a developing historical pattern. New legislation facilitated widespread private citizen involvement, which reinforced international pressure to affect Canadian government policy on the number of Indochinese refugees admitted into Canada. The resettlement picture was further complicated by the distinctive approach of Quebec in contrast to that of other provinces.

It is hoped that this discussion will throw some light on Canadian policy decisions regarding Indochinese refugees.

Background

The Indochinese refugee movement into Canada ranks among the largest since the end of the Second World War. By the end of 1980, this group will constitute about 15 percent of the almost 400,000 displaced and persecuted people welcomed into Canada since 1945, rivalling in the rate of intake two previous large movements. Between 1945 and 1952, Canada took in 186,000 Eastern European refugees. In 1956 and 1957, she received 37,000 Hungarian refugees following the Soviet invasion of that country.

Other special groups created by sudden and unpredictable international crises included: 12,000 Czechs following the Soviet invasion of Czechoslovakia in 1968; 228 Tibetan refugees in 1972 produced by the Chinese takeover of Tibet; 7,000 Ugandan Asians in 1972 following their expulsion by Idi Amin; and 7,000 Latin Americans during the 1970s, the largest single group coming from Chile following the coup d'état in the autumn of 1973.[1]

The groups varied in their cultural affinity with Canadians. With the exception of the Ugandan Asians, most individuals in the other refugee groups did not speak English. But these refugees shared common cultural characteristics and readily adjusted to Canadian life. The Tibetans encountered special problems because their social and cultural heritage was very different from that of other refugee groups and native-born Canadians. The Indochinese refugee group represents a wide diversity of peoples, with many of those from Vietnam sharing the urban and middle-class values of Canadians, while many Laotian refugees are closer to the Tibetan end of the spectrum and encounter greater problems in adjustment.

The Indochinese refugee movement can be compared with other groups not only in size and cultural affinity with Canadians, but with the Czechs and Hungarians who were regarded as fleeing from communism. This ideological factor may have been a consideration in opening our doors to the refugees. If it was a factor, there is no evidence that it was a conscious one, for our investigations have indicated that the ideological issue was neither verbalized nor discussed. This is in stark contrast to the intake of refugees from Czechoslovakia where the ideological issue was

---

1.   Figures come from various brochures issued by Canada Employment and Immigration (DEIC): *Refugee Provisions of the New Canadian Immigration Act Proclaimed April 10, 1978*, July, 1978; *Refugee Settlement Activities 1979*, May, 1979; *Cahier d'exposée traitant du programme d'aide aux réfugiés indochinois*, January, 1980.

clearly very important in the decision to take in Czechs. However, ideology may have been a factor in our judgement that the Indochinese were refugees and not "illegal immigrants," as the Malaysian and Singapore governments labelled them.

As David Wurfel outlines in his chapter, Vietnam was devastated by an armed conflict that lasted thirty years, from 1945 to 1975. The floods and food shortages that followed reunification of the country intensified latent social tensions present in the south of Vietnam since the takeover of Saigon in 1975, particularly when the government attempted to relocate part of the burgeoning urban populace into "new economic zones" in an attempt to make Vietnam self-sufficient in agriculture. The exodus was stimulated by two factors: the increasing tension between China and Vietnam, which began in 1978, and the nationalization measures and currency reform of mid-1978, which hit the Chinese business community hardest.

Meanwhile, Vietnam's involvement in military and para-military activity in Laos and Kampuchea contributed to the migration movement of the inhabitants of those regions, especially those who collaborated with the Americans when they were involved in Indochina. Events accelerated with the Vietnamese occupation of Phnom Penh in January, 1979, and the Chinese border war with Vietnam in February. The 1978 refugee flow, which had receded following the Geneva Conference in December of 1978, turned into a torrent in the spring of 1979.

The indications are that Vietnamese authorities tried to stop refugees from leaving in 1975 to 1977, but the organization of the exodus in 1978 indicated at least semi-official sanction, particularly with regard to the migration of ethnic Chinese in exchange for sums averaging $3,000.[2] Nationalization measures heightened the exodus. The ethnic Chinese within Vietnam, traditionally a suspect group, began to be regarded as aliens as a result of the Vietnamese-Chinese conflict. The motives for leaving, therefore, included a wide gamut of factors, ranging from antipathy to the new economic measures, to ethnic Chinese fear of discrimination, to simple anti-communism.

---

2.   See *Time*, July 30, 1979, pp. 24-27; *Newsweek*, July 2, 1979, pp. 42-50; *Le Nouvel Observateur*, June 25, 1979, pp. 40-42; *Far Eastern Economic Review*, December 22, 1978, pp. 8-13.

Canadian Law and the Designation of the Indochinese as Refugees

The 1976 Immigration Act (proclaimed in April, 1978) finally introduced the concept of a refugee into Canadian legislation, even though Canada had signed the 1951 Geneva Convention in 1969. Before the 1976 act, each refugee movement was treated as an ad hoc problem, with the financial resources available and the population needs of Canada the primary formal considerations in making refugee policy. While recognizing the inability to predict refugee movements, the new law provided for a more efficacious response to international refugee movements.[3]

The law defined a refugee for the first time according to the 1951 Geneva Convention:

"Convention refugee" means any person who, by reason of a well-founded fear of persecution for reasons of race, religion, nationality, membership in a particular social group or political opinion,

(a) is outside the country of his nationality and is unable or, by reason of such fear, is unwilling to avail himself of the protection of that country, or

(b) not having a country or nationality, is outside the country of his former habitual residence and is unable or, by reason of such fear, is unwilling to return to that country.[4]

Prior to 1969, refugees from Communist countries were automatically deemed refugees by our regulations. With the adoption of the United Nations universal definition in 1969, some groups did not fit the legal definition of refugee but were treated as refugees by relaxing our immigration criteria; for example, Moroccan Jews in 1970, Ugandan Asians in 1972, and Chileans in 1973.[5]

The universal definition also proved to be inadequate when dealing with humanitarian movements of people fleeing war zones, such as those fleeing Cyprus and Lebanon during the seventies. As a result, though we had moved closer in legal terms to

3.   DEIC, *Refugee Provisions of the New Canadian Immigration Act Proclaimed April 10, 1978.*

4.   Immigration Act, 1976, article 2.

5.   For example, a cabinet decision was made in 1970 that went beyond the definition in including an oppressed minority group that was still resident in its own country. This was done in order to get the Jews out of Morocco.

the UN formulation, in practice, Canadian operational policy found the UN definition too restrictive.

Thus, even though Parliament now had more to say over refugee immigration movement, the attitude taken to a specific group of refugees was in fact much more open to government discretionary power. This was done by using the designation power of the Immigration Act, namely section 6(2), which allowed the government to decide that a whole class of persons could be defined as refugees under general policies and humanitarian considerations, policies and considerations that are nowhere defined in the act. Therefore, the law increased the role of the governor in council in the inclusion of a group as a designated category of refugees. Section 6(2) provided that, in addition to convention refugees:

any person who is a member of a class *designated* by the Governor in Council as a class, the admission of members of which would be in accordance with Canada's humanitarian tradition with respect to the displaced and the persecuted may be granted admission subject to such regulations as may be established with respect thereto and notwithstanding any other regulations made under this act.[6]

The designated class regulation of December 11, 1978, for Indochinese refugees replaces the convention definition as follows:

"Indochinese Designated Class" means a class of persons the members of which

(a) are citizens or habitual residents of a country listed in the schedule,

(b) have left their country of citizenship or former habitual residence subsequent to April 30, 1975,

(c) have not become permanently resettled,

(d) are unwilling or unable to return to their country of citizenship or former habitual residence,

(e) cannot avail themselves of the protection of any other country, and

(f) are outside Canada and seeking resettlement in Canada.[7]

---

6.   Immigration Act, 1976, section 6(2).

7.   Immigration Act, 1976, Indochinese Designated Class Regulations.

Note, there is no reference to persecution. The definition is subsumed under Canada's humanitarian tradition (section 3). In selecting Indochinese refugees, regulation 4 further removes the normal selection criteria and exempts them from passport requirements. Section 5(1) provides for substitute selection criteria while section 5(2) makes provision for the entry of the refugees under private sponsorship arrangements.[8]

Thus, the bulk of Indochinese were not *formally* Geneva Convention refugees but were identified as a group of refugees under the humanitarian *proviso*.

However, while the government has described its refugee assistance program in humanitarian terms, it is important not to forget the general objectives of the 1976 act which clearly required the policies and regulations to promote Canadian interests domestically and abroad.[9]

The two contrary criteria for defining a refugee — humanitarian grounds and Canadian domestic and foreign self-interest — are mediated by a third one, the legal definition under the 1951 Geneva Convention. The response of Parliament, the provinces, and the public affects the point of balance in this triad of defining factors. The balance, in turn, helps to determine whether a group is to be considered a designated class, the numbers to be allowed in with that class, and the strictness in applying selection procedures to individuals.

Though some of the Indochinese refugees would have qualified as immigrants under the prevailing point system, because these people possessed educational accomplishments and useful skills and were young enough to ensure years of work ahead of them, this was not true of a significant portion of the Indochinese movement. Thus, the weight of consideration had to be given to humanitarian factors. Further, decisions on refugee policy were no

---

8.   Compare these regulations for Indochinese refugees to the ones applied to Latin Americans, who are also designated class refugees. Latin Americans need not have fled their country. On the other hand, they must establish a "well-founded fear of persecution." The third group of designated class refugees, self-exiled East Europeans, have regulations akin to that of the Indochinese. They need not establish fear of persecution and they must be outside their country of origin. In the case of the East European exiles, the clause referring to their "inability to avail themselves of the protection of any other country" is also omitted to prevent Soviet Jews, all of whom carry visas to Israel, from being excluded.

9.   Immigration Act, 1976, article 3.

longer made by simple orders in council but required the plans of the government to be tabled in Parliament following consultation with the provinces. In this way, the decision on the Indochinese refugees was far more open to parliamentary involvement and public debate than had hitherto been the case.

At the same time, the new act provided that any church, corporation, or group of five or more adult Canadian citizens or permanent residents could sponsor a refugee; direct public involvement in the refugee resettlement program was made possible for the first time. And this involvement had an important effect on the numbers of Indochinese refugees brought to Canada.

Canada's Policy on Numbers

Up until the fall of 1976, Canadian refugee attention was focused on Latin America. The Americans, the Australians, and the French were left to deal with the remnants of refugees left from the fall of Saigon, though Canada participated in a residual program in a minor way in order to keep the Canadian presence active as a lever for the United Nations to involve other countries, as well as to provide Canadian expertise in the situation.

By mid-1977 a new exodus of Vietnamese refugees had begun. In the autumn of 1977, the federal cabinet voted to take in fifty families per month. For 1978, this was increased to seventy families per month and included overland refugee families in Thailand that had come from Laos and Kampuchea. Canada arrived at its policy primarily in response to the leading countries engaged in Indochinese refugee work — France, the United States, and Australia. The number of refugees from Indochina admitted into Canada between 1975 and 1978 totalled 9,060.[10]

In the autumn of 1978, the numbers leaving Vietnam began to escalate. Just after the decision to hold a Geneva conference in December, the first very large boat of refugees, the *Hai Hong* with 2,500 refugees aboard, arrived off the coast of Malaysia. The Malaysian navy threatened to push the boat out to sea (see Stubbs, chapter 7). After various consultations, Canada offered to take 600 refugees from the *Hai Hong*. (We actually took 608.) Unlike previous refugee commitments, this decision was made

---

10.   DEIC, *Cahiers d'exposés traitant du programme d'aide aux réfugiés indochinois*, January, 1980, and DEIC, *Annual Report to Parliament on Immigration Levels*, 1980.

without prior cabinet approval. The initiative was well received by both the cabinet and the public.

In the subsequent cabinet discussion, Canada set its refugee quota for 1979 at 10,000, of which 5,000 were reserved for Indochinese refugees and 2,000 were set aside as a contingency. Canada, for the first time, took a leadership role vis-à-vis Indochinese refugees. Further, rather than taking our customary allotment of 10 percent[11] from the *Hai Hong*, Canada opted to take a disproportionate share, both to assure Malaysia that it would not be stuck with refugees and to inspire other countries to participate in assisting in the resettlement program.[12]

By spring of 1979, however, the flow had grown into a torrent. The exodus, which previously averaged 5,000 per month, rose to 51,000 in May. In June there were almost 57,000. By the end of July, the total numbers who had left Vietnam by boat totalled over 290,000.[13]

On the recommendation of the minister of Employment and Immigration and the minister of External Affairs, the cabinet voted to incease the quota for Indochinese refugees from 5,000 to 8,000 by allotting the contingency figure of 2,000 to the Indochinese and adding an additional 1,000 from the immigration quota. This policy, announced on June 22, was arrived at with considerably more discussion than had been the previous custom.

For the first time, a target of 4,000 refugees was set for the private sector. As noted, the new Immigration Act, passed the previous year, introduced an innovative provision that permitted churches, corporations, or groups of five or more adult Canadian citizens or permanent residents to sponsor refugees directly. By announcing the target, the government hoped the public would become more aware of the new vehicle because, until that time, with few exceptions (such as the Mennonites), most of the large churches had been reluctant to utilize the proviso lest it be used by

---

11.   Interview with Kirk Bell, Deputy Executive Director of Immigration and Demographic Policy with special responsibility for refugees.

12.   There were precedents for Canada taking such initiative. In 1975 Canadians took a disproportionate share of Soviet Jews stranded in Belgium and of Soviet Jews who were in Rome in 1977. In the latter case, since those Jews had stopped for a short period in Israel, they were not officially refugees, but Canada's initiative helped clear up the remnants of Jews left in Rome.

13.   Office of the UNHCR, *Meeting on Refugees and Displaced Persons in Southeast Asia: Note by the High Commissioner*, 1979.

the government to dump its responsibilities for refugees on to the private sector.

The June decision to set a government quota of 8,000 and a target for the private sector of 4,000 was part of the already established policy of attempting to relieve the anxiety of the front-line nations which were receiving the refugees, while setting an example for other countries to emulate. In the meantime, two new initiatives were introduced by the Department of External Affairs. An attempt was made to broaden the range of participating countries. At the same time, pressure was placed on Vietnam to stem the refugee tide at the source.

In a joint communiqué of External Affairs and Immigration of June 21, 1979, Vietnam was accused of abusing the international moral order in flagrant and continuous violation of human rights.[14] Secretary of State for External Affairs Flora MacDonald, in a speech in Geneva on July 20, accused Vietnam of brutal oppression and outrageous abuse of fundamental human rights. At the same time, she tried to navigate between the Scylla of the right of every human to leave his country of origin and the Charybdis of trying to stem the flow at the source. She criticized Vietnam for its expulsion of an entire community and socio-economic class. Canada, MacDonald proclaimed, was not asserting this on political or economic grounds but strictly on humanitarian principles, as if Canada's predominant ideology had absolutely nothing to do with the stand.[15]

The incorporation of broader foreign policy goals into Indochinese refugee policy was paralleled on the domestic front by the appearance of an equally novel phenomenon — the development of the private sponsorship movement. As an example, within two weeks of the inception of Operation Lifeline by the private sector in Ontario on June 24, 1979, sixty chapters of Operation Lifeline had sprung up all over the province.

Since the government June figures had designated 8,000 government-sponsored refugees and set a target of 4,000 privately sponsored ones, some elements in the private sector had proposed that for every privately sponsored refugee above 4,000, the govern-

---

14. DEIC and Secretary of State for External Affairs (SSEA), *Déclaration conjointe*, June 20, 1979.

15. *Notes pour une allocution du SEAE devant la Conférence des Nations-Unies sur les réfugiés à Genève*, July 20, 1979.

ment would agree to take two additional publicly sponsored refugees above 8,000. The cabinet introduced a bold new variation of this idea as a matching formula, promising to take in an additional 21,000 refugees on a one-to-one basis for every refugee sponsored by the private sector to a total of 21,000. The target to the end of 1980 was set at 50,000.[16]

Instead of taking eighteen months to reach the 21,000 target, the private sector surpassed that number by the end of four months. The cabinet was faced with a problem. Should the 50,000 target of 1980 be broken by allowing the private sector to reach its natural level? Or should private sponsorships be cut off? Or should the matching formula be halted so that the government would take only the balance of 50,000 refugees not privately sponsored? The latter idea was adopted, assisted by the need to find funds to assist refugees from Kampuchea. The cabinet decided that the 50,000 figure was a delicate symbol; breaking through the barrier would greatly enhance the backlash movement and endanger the whole program. The decision was made to use the funds saved from government sponsorships (approximately $1,300 per refugee)[17] for Cambodian relief.

Church spokesmen and leaders of private sponsorship organizations claimed the government reneged on its promise. The growth of private sponsorship was not supposed to affect government efforts. The shift in policy was loudly denounced by the opposition. When the Liberals returned to power in February of 1980, private sponsorships had been arranged for 35,000. It was clear that, under the old formula, the government would not be sponsoring any Indochinese refugees in 1980. The new government pledged to take in an additional 10,000 government-sponsored refugees in 1980.

To make up for the increased load on the private sector, part of the savings of cancelling the matching formula ($1,310,000) was allotted to aid voluntary organizations involved in assisting Indochinese refugee resettlement in Canada. The sum of $710,000 was made available to co-ordinating organizations backing up private sponsors to assist in administrative costs, while $600,000 was made available to private agencies for interpretation, escort, and orientation services to the refugees themselves. An earlier initiative

16.   DEIC and SSEA, *Déclaration conjointe*, July 18, 1979.

17.   DEIC, *Bulletin réfugiés indochinois*, December 13, 1979, p. 13.

of the previous summer was the inauguration of the Canada Refugee Foundation with an initial grant of $410,000.

Canada's Selection Policy

The humanitarian rhetoric and the large public involvement combined with international pressures to affect our application of selection criteria in the light of the stated Canadian self-interest objectives of the act. Even the decision to take in the large figure of 50,000 Indochinese refugees is compatible with the self-interest factor when the context of the total net level of immigration is taken into account.

In 1980, for example, the federal government plans to take in a total of 120,000 immigrants, which includes about 25,000 Indochinese refugees. Since 75,000 people emigrate from Canada every year, the net immigration flow to Canada, for 1980, numbers only 45,000.[18] And when we take into consideration the fall in the birthrate to a point below a figure sufficient to maintain the Canadian population, the net immigration rate barely manages to prevent Canada from suffering from a decline in population.

This mixture of humanitarianism and self-interest also affects the selection process. Immigrants have to obtain a certain score in a point system that is used to evaluate an applicant's capacity to care for and maintain himself and his dependants in adapting to a productive role in Canada. Officials continue to use the point system in evaluating refugee applicants but apply it in a relaxed way; refugees are not excluded simply because they are not able to muster sufficient points. The basic considerations are whether the individual is a true refugee under the Geneva Convention on the designated class provision and whether the person has the potential to settle successfully in Canada.

The evaluation of the potential to settle successfully depended primarily on the immigration officer's interpretation of "motives."

No one factor, with the exception of personal motivation is a mandatory criterion for admission to Canada. Personal motivation is assessed in a general way, taking into account such things as personal success in their own country, independent of whether they have worked as tradesmen, artisans, labourers or professionals.[19]

---

18.   DEIC, *Annual Report to Parliament on Immigration Levels*, 1980, p. 34(15).

19.   DEIC, *Newsletter: Indochinese Refugees*, July 24, 1979, p. 7.

That interpretation of motive relies on past success independent of the particular occupation in which the refugee achieved such success. But the success of a farmer or fisherman cannot be measured in the same way as that of a lawyer or teacher, so it is difficult to understand how immigration officers make such judgements. It would seem, in fact, that socio-economic factors might play an important part in assessing the potential success of a Vietnamese lawyer, say, in comparison to that of a fisherman, for the individual could be interpreted as having skills and a strong motive for upward mobility that might determine greater "success" in Canadian terms.

Many Canadians, particularly church leaders, have criticized this policy as too inhumane towards fatherless families and families burdened with sick and handicapped people. A prominent Dutch official accused Canada of skimming the cream off the top.[20] The countries of first asylum feared that they, as poor countries least able to provide assistance, would be left with the weak and the maimed. However, since health, education, and welfare are primarily provincial responsibilities, the co-operation of the provincial authorities is essential in providing assistance for problem cases. Thus, joint assistanceship programs worked out between churches and the federal government must also involve the assent of provincial authorities.

The Specific Role of the Province of Quebec

If divided jurisdiction between the federal government and the provinces complicates the application of humanitarian considerations in the selection process, the unique role of Quebec also has to be mentioned in understanding the resettlement of refugees in Canada. In the present constitutional context of Canada, the sector of immigration represents a shared jurisdiction between federal government and provincial governments. Thus, the federal government and the provincial governments play a role in supervising and administering immigration processes.

Historically, provinces were generally not active in selecting and sponsoring refugees. Without any doubt, Quebec has been the most involved in formulating a complete immigration policy, especially since the Parti Québécois assumed power in 1976. Estimating that a systematic intervention in the sector of immi-

---

20.   Richard Wilson, "A Case of Eeny, Meeny, Miney, No," *Macleans*, November 5, 1979, p. 35.

gration constitutes a powerful instrument of demographic control, the Québécois government aims to obtain more autonomy in this field of action.

In this respect, February, 1978, was an important landmark for the government of Canada and that of Quebec: an agreement was signed (the Couture-Cullen Agreement) on forms of collaboration for immigration strategy and on the selection process of individuals wanting to resettle in Quebec.[21] This agreement includes a section on federal-provincial collaboration in relation to refugees. On the one hand, this document states that refugee selection has to be conducted on the basis of co-operation between the government of Ottawa and the government of Quebec, thereby giving Quebec a unique role relative to that of other provinces. On the other hand, the document states that refugee adaptation should be a provincial responsibility, which is consistent with the responsibilities other provinces have assumed.

In brief, Quebec recognizes that the admission of refugees into the country should be decided by the federal government only, accepts that their selection be made on the basis of co-operation, and agrees that their adaptation is a strictly provincial responsibility. Since a refugee sponsorship program involves the adaptation process, Quebec feels it is its duty to establish its own refugee sponsorship program.

Quebec's sponsorship program is very similar to the federal government's except on a few points. The federal government accepts sponsorships from corporations, whereas the provincial government of Quebec does not. Moreoover, Quebec gave out $400 grants to the first 300 sponsorship applications channelled to the provincial Department of Immigration.

At first sight, some statistics may suggest that Quebec welcomes proportionally fewer refugees than other provinces. By February, 1980, Quebec had sponsored 4,890 refugees, whereas Ontario had sponsored 15,042.[22] However, these figures are misleading because they do not show the governmental involvement of the province of Quebec.

---

21.   Ministère de l'immigration du Québec, *Entente entre le gouvernement du Canada et le gouvernement du Québec portant sur la collaboration en matière d'immigration*, February, 1978.

22.   DEIC, *Newsletter: Indochinese Refugees*, February 14, 1980, app. p. 2.

The government of Quebec has taken the decision of directly sponsoring 10,000 refugees in addition to refugees sponsored by private groups in Quebec. This provincial initiative is unique in Canada and it will allow Quebec to receive, by the end of 1980, approximately 16,000 refugees from Southeast Asia. Thus, whereas the private sponsorship program has had a greater impact in other Canadian provinces, Quebec is using a different formula in order to play its role in the re-establishment of Southeast Asian refugees.

Conclusion

Without undercutting the role of humanitarian factors in government refugee policy, other forces have clearly been of significant import — international pressures, domestic public involvement, religious concerns, and provincial-federal relations. With the exception of those in the public who oppose the intake of Third World immigrants, most other factors — humanitarianism, self-interest, the involvement of the public and the provinces — combine to facilitate a larger intake of refugees, although the public and provincial sectors have not been as compatible in ensuring a program for needy cases. Given the publicity over the trials and ordeals of this refugee group, there has been virtually no challenge to the judgement in Canada that these people are legitimate refugees.

All things considered, it would be wrong to stigmatize the federal government response to the refugee issue as merely a reaction to domestic pressures[23] or even international pressures. The federal government demonstrated leadership, as did the provincial government in Quebec. The Canadian public and the international community encouraged that leadership and showed an overwhelming, positive response to it, and this response better enabled and indeed pressured the government in turn to increase the quantitative intake and take steps to provide special attention for needy cases.

It is a unique example of co-operation and interaction in the public and private sectors and in provincial-federal relations.

---

23.   *The Boat People: An "Age" Investigation with Bruce Grant* (London: Penguin Books, 1979), p. 174.

Young boy reflecting on his situation in Malaysian camp.

Language class enjoying traditional maple syrup party in Quebec.

10

Cultural Factors Affecting the Adjustment of Southeast Asian Refugees

by
Penny Van Esterik

Introduction

When sponsors or refugees talk about adjustment problems, they invariably refer to the weather, the food, and of course the culture. Seldom do they explain exactly what cultural differences cause the endless series of misinterpretations or communication difficulties associated with contact between people steeped in two vastly different cultural systems. Sponsors, sponsoring agencies, and refugees would probably be hard pressed to define exactly what they meant by cultural differences. For as soon as we try to spell out differences in values or patterns of personal interaction, we recognize the stereotypes we are creating and the overgeneralizations we are perpetuating in the name of "understanding."

In full appreciation of the inevitable distortions that are born of over-simplification, to say nothing of the pitfalls facing an author who writes generally about a complex subject, I nonetheless undertook this chapter in the hope that my experience as an anthropologist in Southeast Asia and as a sponsor of a refugee family might clarify some of these cultural differences for others.[1]

Culture

A brief description of Southeast Asian societies should highlight the differences between these societies and our own. We want to know how the world looks to the refugees through the "invisible framework" that gives meaning to their lives. This invisible framework, or "glasses," is culture, systems of shared ideas underlying the ways in which people live. A recent textbook in cultural anthropology explains it this way:

It is as though we . . . grow up perceiving the world through glasses with distorting lenses. The things, events, and relationships we assume to be "out there" are in fact filtered through this perceptual screen. The first reaction, inevitably, on encountering people who wear a different kind of glasses is to dismiss their behaviour as strange or wrong. . . Although we can never take our glasses off to find out what the world is "really like," or try looking through anyone else's without ours on as well, we can at least learn a good deal about our own prescription.[2]

Although the Laotians, Cambodians, and Vietnamese settling in North American communities may quickly change their observable behaviour, they will continue to view their world through their own glasses. In fact, most refugees will adjust to their new homes long before they completely understand the cultural differences, learn new cultural patterns, or put aside their vivid memories of life in Cambodia, Laos, and Vietnam. Cultural change is not a mysterious process but something that allows us to adapt to our changing world as well. People use their experience and their assumptions about the world to help them make sense out of that world, bearing in mind the inevitable distortions inherent in the task.

Who are the Refugees?

In earlier chapters of this book we learn who the refugees are, where they come from, and what historical and political

---

1.   Most of my experience has been with Laotian and Cambodian refugees; some of my generalities may not apply to Vietnamese refugees.

2.   Roger M. Keesing, *Cultural Anthropology* (New York: Holt, Rinehart and Winston, 1976) p. 139.

events pushed them from their homes into the refugee camps and beyond. Their social and cultural identity is equally important. We need to recognize some of the differences among refugees so that we avoid stereotypic responses to their needs and problems. Just as there is no "typical Canadian," there is no "typical refugee." They are members of a category, *refugee*, but with the exception of that common status, they may have little else in common. The refugees have faced great personal and material losses, and they have also lost their countries — the contact with their land and national heritage, which may mean more to some people than others. They inevitably will grieve for their losses both privately and collectively, and nothing the sponsor can do will change that fact. At best, sponsors can help the refugees express their grief in socially acceptable ways.

The refugees also lack control over their own lives. While some Vietnamese refugees in 1975 made a conscious choice to leave an intolerable situation, many Cambodians and Laotians were pushed by the threat of starvation and imminent death into Thailand or Malaysia. And from that point on, they all were part of a process that they were almost powerless to influence. Waiting for security, sponsorship, and transportation, they shared the inevitable feeling of powerlessness.

The refugees from Southeast Asia exhibit a wide range of ethnic, occupational, and educational differences. Some occupational differences may be based on ethnic tradition. The better-educated, wealthier professionals are more likely to have descended from Chinese families, even though their present ethnic identification is Lao, Khmer, or Vietnamese. Smaller numbers of Hmong or Meo tribesmen from Laos are also seeking refuge in other countries. These proud and egalitarian opium farmers differ significantly from the Lao, Khmer, and Vietnamese (see Indra, chapter 11). Sponsoring communities might receive refugees who were university educated, wealthy, and influential in their homelands, or refugees who were illiterate in their own languages, unfamiliar with Western-style technology, and living on a bare subsistence level. The problems faced by these two kinds of refugees are quite distinct, and the problems faced by the sponsors of each correspondingly different.

Consider first the Vietnamese businessman or the Cambodian doctor forced by circumstances to enter refugee status. These men or women may be literate and well educated but unable to speak and write English. They may be expected to study English as a second language with illiterate peasant farmers who have never written their native language. The educated refugees face the additional humiliation of being unable to practise their vocation. The doctor who must learn English or French and upgrade medical skills may take a job as an orderly or work at any unskilled job to earn money. Although this experience may be common to other immigrants, it is particularly difficult for Southeast Asians with well-developed notions of hierarchy and social status. It is sometimes hard for sponsors to realize that the exhausted, confused refugee, dressed in mismatched clothes from a charitable organization, used to dress in the latest Japanese fashions, wear more gold jewellery than many of us have seen, and drive an imported car.

The sponsor's initial task is quite simple, as these refugees would be familiar with Western technology, knowledgeable about banks, hospitals, and bureaucracies, and highly motivated to enrol their children or themselves in school programs. Yet, they may be particularly uncomfortable taking instructions and more frustrated at the lack of control they have over their lives. As patrons in Southeast Asia, they will be uncomfortable assuming the role of a dependent client in their new homeland, and their self-esteem may suffer accordingly.

Compare those refugees with the Vietnamese fisherman and the Lao peasant rice farmer, both living, as 80 percent of Southeast Asians live, in rural villages, working hard to provide sufficient food for their families and seldom producing substantial surplus to convert to cash. (Many Southeast Asian peasant families have an annual cash income under $200.)

These latter refugees face a different set of problems once they settle in their new homeland. The trip to North America and the contact with Western communities would be most unsettling, since there would be nothing in their past experience to aid them in this new cultural context.

For these refugees, the language classes and the voluminous supplies of written instructions, manuals, advice, and booklets on their new country may be confusing. Unaccustomed to receiving and processing written information, they may take longer to orient themselves to a classroom situation.

The sponsors of such refugees have many different problems. These newcomers have moved into a world of material wealth and complexity. They may be unfamiliar with electricity, stoves, refrigerators, and all the luxuries of a North American life-style. Sponsors may be treated as generous patrons giving so much to their clients that the clients worry about how they will ever repay their obligation. A peasant farmer from Laos resettled in a middle-sized city may find janitorial or restaurant work provides him with an opportunity to demonstrate his worth, learn new skills, and practise his new language. At the same time, he will increase his self-esteem by performing well under difficult circumstances (see Buchignani, chapter 12).

We are familiar with differences in socio-economic status, and most of us interact with people who are poor as well as people who are relatively wealthy. What, then, is the difference in the context of Southeast Asian societies? How can we tie these social factors in with the more abstract notions of cultural values as we try to understand the subtleties of Southeast Asian social structure?

Status and Hierarchy

Vietnamese, Lao, and Khmer languages all make many distinctions regarding relative social superiority and inferiority. Ideas of hierarchy and social inequality are subtly expressed in many ways in Southeast Asia. From the sumptuary laws, which proscribed the wearing of certain garments and jewellery for different statuses in the ancient Lao and Khmer kingdoms, to the fine distinctions in titles and rank, which characterized the Vietnamese Confucian public service examinations, there is a long tradition behind the idea that people have a definite place in the social order. Knowing where you fit tells you how to behave when interacting with other people, and what is expected of you. Fear that they will not know what is expected of them is a real concern to Southeast Asian refugees. This point was clearly brought home to me in Thailand as I overheard a young Lao stammering on the telephone. Usually she chatted comfortably, but because she was unsure of the age and social status of the person she was addressing, she could not communicate. Once she knew this information, she spoke effortlessly, secure in the knowledge that she was using the correct pronouns.

To understand the differences between the Laotian rice farmer and the Vietnamese businessman, we should explore the nature of the patron-client relationship in Southeast Asia.

The patron-client relationship refers to a one-to-one personal contact between two persons, one the patron, who is hierarchically superior to the other, the client. This is the characteristic social relationship in Southeast Asia whether the social unit is a family, a village, a religious community, or a government bureaucracy. People do not perceive themselves as simply members of a social class but rather as a part of a set of interlocking patron-client relationships. A person will be a patron to some people, a client to others. The relationship involves an expectation of reciprocity; that is, any thing or favour given must be reciprocated. In a village setting, patrons may give rice to clients, while clients will return political support or labour to the patron. In bureaucracies, the patron may have the characteristics of a mentor. However, patron-client relations tend to be brittle. Clients are always seeking patrons who may have more to give in terms of wealth and power. Patrons try to keep clients and to find more, but they are not surprised if clients melt away when their ability to supply goods or service fades. However, the relationship may be broken if patrons fail or if other patrons seem to provide better opportunities. Laotians, Vietnamese, and Cambodians are known for their mobility and adaptability. A social structure and organization based on this patron-client relationship explains, in part, this ability.

For the sponsor or sponsoring group, many interpersonal difficulties could be avoided by trying to understand where particular refugees fitted in the complex networks of patron-client relations that existed in their communities in Southeast Asia. Similar relations may easily re-emerge in the new social structures being constructed in their new homeland. Since construction of new patron-client relationships takes place all the time in Southeast Asia, it is likely that this process will continue here. The sponsor should be aware of this network of relationships of which he is now a part. As a patron, he or she is part of a set of interrelated obligations that are not specified but are real enough for the refugee. It is not unusual for refugees to discuss and compare their sponsors, and even negotiate for a change in sponsorship, if it appears to be to their advantage. (This may leave the sponsor feeling extremely confused, to say the least.)

Age Differences

Refugees of all ages will be resettling in North America. On a cliché level, we say that the young ones will adjust best and the old ones will "never really change." Behind this statement is a range of assumptions about age differences which deserve more careful examination.

Infants born into Southeast Asian families are welcomed with love and indulgence. They are seldom allowed to cry, and older children — both boys and girls — may cuddle their new sibling for hours while doing other tasks. Needless to say, babies are very happy and content. My Cambodian friend was very disturbed as she watched a young Western mother leave an infant to cry lest she "spoil" the child. Yet a child may be displaced at two or three years of age as a new baby arrives. The three-year-old may be weaned abruptly and put into the care of an older sibling or other relative. Southeast Asian children are experienced sibling care-takers and are well able to accept the responsibility for this task. A young Laotian woman discussing her relation to her siblings said that she loved one sister more than all others because she "raised" her. This bond was stronger than the bond between other siblings. Such bonds continue through life and may explain close relation-ships among siblings that continue in the new country. The relations between brothers and sisters are also defined through kinship terms that distinguish between older and younger siblings. Thus, a younger brother owes respect and deference to his older sister, and his younger brother would refer to him with terms indicating deference (see Royle, chapter 3). These distinctions of relative age (older and younger) carry over into school where a Grade 3 student owes respect and deference to a Grade 4 student. Hence the problems that may develop if siblings of different ages are all placed in the same school grade.

This hierarchical order between siblings and the associated terms of address and reference may be used to define relationships for the refugees in offices, factories, or government offices where relative age and seniority explain, in part, social interaction. In a way, an elder is like a patron, so that even a poor farmer, a client to a great many people, is at least a patron for his children and younger siblings.

We may be struck by the independence of Southeast Asian children and the ease with which parents teach by example rather than by coercion. While I would insist that my seven-year-old daughter eat cereal and wear her boots, a Cambodian mother living with us watched her children drink coke and eat cake for breakfast and leave the house in sandals in winter, secure in the knowledge that they would soon come to realize that was not appropriate behaviour and would make the change. They soon did learn this, while I still am unable to let my daughter learn by experience and tend to give her direct instructions.

The independence of children is further seen in the ease with which a parent may give away a child to live with another relative. A Lao mother may state quite matter-of-factly that her daughter never listened to her, but she was very compatible with her aunt, who had no daughter, and so she "became" her mother. It is a matter of who is to be the child's patron, and children learn to reciprocate in the relationship so that aunt becomes mother. In parts of Southeast Asia, this flexibility in family composition is common and infants may be given away to relatives at birth.[3] It will not be compatible with our Western notions of fixed, family structure, parent-child relations, or our legal system.

Respect for the elderly, is a widely accepted value in Southeast Asian societies. This respect extends to the very oldest members of a family who were probably living within the family compound in the Southeast Asian context. Children reciprocate the care and love given to them when they were helpless and dependent infants by extending this care to their aged parents. Some children as adults may choose to ignore their parents, but they would be criticized for not showing respect or reciprocating the care they received. There are social sanctions for not reciprocating nourishing or supporting behaviour. For example, a child who shuns good parents is also a person who may not reciprocate patrons or clients. His social capital would then be at a very low ebb.

In Laos and Cambodia, the support of elderly parents may be the responsibility of the youngest daughter, who may live with her aged parents, care for them, and, in turn, inherit the house and some land. In Vietnam, this is usually the responsibility of the youngest son. Elders are consulted about family business matters, mediate in family squabbles, and generally guide the direction of family decisions, particularly when they still control the land. In extended family households, they are especially important in arranging marriages and caring for grandchildren. They retain some of this influence after their deaths, when, as

---

3.   Strong sibling relations, extended families, and polygamy are less common in Vietnam than in Laos and Cambodia, and a Vietnamese parent would only give away a baby under conditions of dire poverty.

ancestors, they deserve respect — both formal (in Vietnamese society) and informal (in Laotian and Cambodian societies).

Sponsors should be particularly wary of usurping the authority and influence of senior family members. For example, a Vietnamese civil servant, no longer the productive breadwinner, might find his influence diminishing in his family as the sponsor guides his children through the intricacies of school registration and provides them with clothes. Or an elderly Laotian couple are set up in their own apartment so as not to strain the meagre resources of their daughter and her young family; this leaves the daughter distressed that she is not fulfilling her duty to her parents, while the parents feel lonely, useless, and unable to provide the guidance their daughter needs. Nevertheless, sponsors need not allow these cultural differences to interfere with their responsibilities for the refugees' welfare.

A greater problem is the single refugee without family, all of the members being dead or left behind in the country of origin. These individuals face deeper despair and require careful and sensitive assistance as they face the task of acculturation alone. If possible, it is useful to resettle these single persons in areas where there are other refugees with whom they can associate.

Sex Roles

The adjustment problems for Southeast Asian refugees will differ for males and females. It is important to understand sex role differences in Southeast Asian societies in order to understand their preconceptions about males and females.

When speaking of sex roles, we must include the opportunities available to women in particular cultural contexts, and also how women are defined. That is, it makes little sense to say that women have a high status because they are doctors, lawyers, or politicians, if women are devalued or considered polluting or worthless. Generally, Western stereotypes of Asians are more favourable to Southeast Asian women (delicate, feminine) than the Southeast Asian men, who may be viewed as weak or unmasculine.

Southeast Asian women have relatively high status compared to women in India and traditional China. They are doctors, lawyers, bank presidents, shop and hotel owners, real estate tycoons, professors, civil servants, and market peddlars, to name but a few of the occupations filled by women. This does not mean that women are not exploited and discriminated against in some domains. But it should sensitize us to the fact that many refugee women were competent professionals or entrepreneurs in the public domain before becoming refugees. Women are considered competent, enterprising, and often more rational or calculating in financial matters than men. Men tend to be the indulgent spenders in a family — the consumers of major goods — while women are more often frugal, shrewd, and concerned with the material welfare of the family.

Marriages in Southeast Asia are generally arranged by the parents of the bride and groom. Although some modern marriages are based on romantic love, the best marriage is said to be between "friends." The marriage relation carries fewer expectations and responsibilities compared to Western marriages. For example, husbands and wives generally go to parties and visit friends separately. It is not unusual for men in some Southeast Asian countries to have a second wife if they can support one. This need not break up the first marriage, particularly if the marriage was carefully arranged by the parents of both parties and if there are children. It is not at all unusual for several men to spend an evening drinking together and visiting prostitutes. While such behaviour might shatter a Western marriage, a Southeast Asian woman once shrugged the matter off lightly, saying, "That is what men are like."

In Lao and Khmer communities, both men and women may inherit land or goods, and it is quite common for a husband to move in with his wife's family. But in Vietnam, it is more usual for women to move to their husband's compound and descent is traced patrilineally through clans. Vietnamese women have fewer rights, even in the new Communist regime where women have less educational and political opportunities and receive fewer work points than men. But, in spite of differences in family and political structure, Southeast Asian women regularly achieve positions of economic and professional power that North American women might envy. What makes this possible?

Many Southeast Asian households include grandparents or cousins who can help a working mother continue her activities outside the home. Alternatively, a family could "adopt" a young girl from a poor rural family to meet the domestic and child care responsibilities usually performed by women. In addition, both male and female teenaged children may be expected to take care of domestic responsibilities when their mothers are working elsewhere.

In many North American communities, substantial educational and career opportunities are made available to male refugees. At the same time, the women may face an unfamiliar pattern of isolation in a nuclear family with young children. Nothing is expected of them except that they perform as good wives and mothers. Where formerly they defined themselves by their work in the public domain, in their new communities they may find few outlets for their entrepreneurial skills. What of the market woman, the rice-mill operator, the peasant woman who evaluated rice seeds, planted, harvested, and negotiated the sale of the rice crops? How will she adapt to the isolation and limited expectations quite normal for a North American wife and mother? Or will Southeast Asian women bring new inspiration to North American women seeking equality and opportunity in the public domain?

Health and Nutrition

Many refugees may arrive in North America with serious medical problems. Naturally, these problems will be dealt with according to modern standards of biomedical care, and the medical beliefs of the patient are largely irrelevent when emergency care is given. Nevertheless, it may be useful to keep in mind some common cultural assumptions about health care.

Doctors are respected and generally trusted, but to many Southeast Asians living outside major cities, hospitals are places where you go to die. The only way to survive a hospital stay would be to have family members in attendance at all times. Injections are generally well understood and treated as almost magical cures. Medication may be mistreated; if one pill is beneficial, then maybe four pills will be four times as beneficial.

In traditional Southeast Asian medical systems, herbal drinks are widely used, particularly by women. These mixtures may increase strength and remove symptoms of fatigue. Since these drinks are no longer available to them, a nutritious substitute may be found, which older men and women may appreciate.

Southeast Asian women are usually quite knowledgeable about birth control and aware of the benefits of family planning, although they may be unwilling to discuss this with a male physician.

The mental health of the refugees is a matter of great concern to sponsors, but it is an area where few generalizations are possible.

Without doubt, all refugees must feel stress and depression as they realize the extent of their losses and the magnitude of the adjustment they must make to North American communities. Most refugees have lost both the social support of family and community and the spiritual support of a religious system, such as Buddhism. (Although there are attempts to re-establish Laotian and Cambodian monastic traditions, these efforts affect only a few refugees. Many refugees saw respected monks killed along with lay people.)

Some individuals may be unable to handle the stress and depression themselves. For a few, their response might be psychosomatic illnesses, trance, violence, or even suicide (see Suh, chapter 13). No Western mental health services can provide the kind of therapies traditionally practised in Southeast Asia, where spirits can be exorcized, amulets provided for protection, and wandering souls tied back securely to ease troubled minds. Few communities could provide such rituals for refugees in North America. At present, the best protection is an open, honest love expressed in ways that transcend cultural boundaries.

Another survival problem that is quickly negotiated is food. Although there are many potential problems around food, sponsors seldom mention this as an area of great concern to them or the refugees. Because of differences among individuals and families, there may be a wide range of acceptable food alternatives. One surprised sponsor learned, after purchasing 100 pounds of rice, that the Vietnamese family staying with her did not like rice. With allowances for the many individual food habits, it is still possible to describe widely shared food patterns in Southeast Asia.

Cities like Vientiane, Phnom Penh, and Saigon were cosmopolitan centres where the best of international cuisine was available. For the wealthy urban dweller, the French legacy provided European specialty foods. Even the poor could afford the long loaves of French bread made locally. A startled sponsor heard two Cambodian women express their disappointment over supermarket baked goods, since they had lived beside a *patisserie* run by a French-trained baker in a Cambodian town.

For most of mainland Southeast Asia, the diet centres around rice, fish, and vegetables, with other meat dishes available to wealthier families. Boiled white rice is the staple cereal food. Unfortunately, the mechanical milling procedures guarantee the whitest rice by removing the vitamin-rich bran. Brown rice, fed to prisoners and soldiers, is a very low-status food. Lao prefer the glutinous rice, steamed in a basket and formed easily into small balls.

Dried fish and fermented fish sauce are staples for the majority of Southeast Asian peasant farmers. Pork, chicken, and beef provide the basis of side dishes for wealthier families. These meats are rare in many households more for economic reasons than for moral reasons, as the Buddhist injunction against killing can be circumvented — and fish, too, must be killed. (Actually they are removed from the water and left to die of their own accord.) Most vegetables are prepared by the fast-fry method, which conserves both fuel and the vitamin and mineral content of these foods. Vegetables may be preserved by pickling or fermenting. Hot sauces made with chili peppers are usually served separately so that individuals may determine how spicy they want their dish. Noodles are a common substitute for rice, particularly at noon meals.

Foods are always served in a culturally determined pattern. In Southeast Asian societies, the same dishes may be served with rice for breakfast, lunch, or dinner. In North America, breakfast may consist of toast and jam, but noodles or last night's left-overs are perfectly appropriate in refugee households.

An evening meal of rice and side dishes may be prepared in the afternoon, covered, and kept until individual family members are hungry. Most side dishes are acceptable when cold or luke-warm. The family may not feel comfortable sitting down formally together and discussing the day's activities. Meals are much more relaxed and informal than North American meals. If an individual is not hungry, there is no pressure to eat with "the family," although food may be left for him or her. Dishes are shared, but it is considered impolite for two people to serve themselves from a common dish at the same time. Unlike our pattern of laying out food one course at a time in a fixed order, Southeast Asian meals present all available alternatives at once, and the individual determines the order in which specific dishes are eaten. Fruit is generally not eaten with meals but between meals as a snack. If at all possible, family members prefer to bathe before eating the evening meal. To many, it is more important to bathe before eating than to eat a meal together.

As in all societies, food is imbued with meaning and these meanings help determine what foods will be eaten in certain circumstances. Generally, rice is the focus of a meal, and if rice is not consumed, the family members are not full. Food is part of the system of disease causation widespread in Southeast Asia. Certain foods have medicinal qualities needed to cure certain diseases or conditions. In addition, foods are classified as hot or cold, and these properties determine what foods can be consumed at certain times. These are not thermal values but properties intrinsic to certain foods. Although this is part of a traditional pattern of disease causation, it is perfectly possible to combine biomedical aspects of disease causation with careful selection of food based on the hot/cold dichotomy.

The refugees may have problems that are associated with their food. For example, many individuals and families may be badly nourished from weeks and months of food shortages in Cambodia or shortages during their escape. Although the refugee camps in Southeast Asia must alleviate these initial states of malnutrition, the refugees may still exhibit some symptoms of malnutrition and anxieties about food. These conditions may affect other health problems of refugees.

Problems could also arise from the fact that most Southeast Asians are intolerant to lactose, the sugar in milk products. Children over four and adults do not have the enzyme, lactase, to enable them to digest milk products. Drinking milk may cause cramps and diarrhea. Some doctors argue that by introducing small amounts of milk into the diet, an individual may gradually come to tolerate milk products. Many refugees may try milk with sugar and flavouring, since the taste of milk is not a pleasant or familiar one to most of them. Western doctors may be unaware of the seriousness of lactose intolerance and prescribe milk as an accompaniment to certain drugs. This may complicate the cure considerably.

Finally, sponsors and agencies interested in the welfare of refugees must recognize that it is possible for refugees to suffer from real nutritional problems in North America. In most cases, they will not lack calories, and sufficient food will be available to them. Nevertheless, through lack of experience in supermarket shopping and the availability of nutritionally inadequate food, refugees can easily suffer a drop in nutritional health.

Refugees who survived in Southeast Asia on rice, fish sauce, and vegetables may shift to a diet of white bread, coke, and cookies. The tremendous range of food alternatives available in North

American stores provides opportunities for some remarkably poor nutritional choices. Since children are generally permitted to choose their own foods, it is unlikely that parents would step in to remove highly valued treats like soda pop, candy, cookies, doughnuts, and so forth, from their children. Sponsors who attempt to keep this kind of food from the refugees will probably encounter much resistance and appear cheap and mean.

It is an important task for the sponsor or agency to communicate some of the nutritional traps in our food markets and demonstrate by example how a meal as balanced as rice, fish sauce, and vegetables can be obtained in North America.

Communication

Most refugee problems can be related in some way to communication in its broadest sense. It is difficult for people who have never experienced the sensation of not understanding any of the words spoken around them to appreciate the loneliness and fear the refugees must feel. Even with a few words of English and some ability to anticipate questions, much of the meaning of on-going dialogue will be lost. This disorientation must be particularly uncomfortable for individuals who like to have others understand their intentions or feelings as clearly as possible.

As fluency in English or French increases, refugees may use their language skills in ways that could upset Westerners. For example, the first questions that are asked may be considered quite personal. How old are you? Why do you have only one child? How much did you pay for your shirt, TV, cake? These questions are not meant to be insulting, and Southeast Asians constantly ask them of each other. Because of our sense of privacy and our reluctance to discuss personal finances, we may find these questions rude. (I respond by saying that I forgot the exact price — a foolish thing for a woman to do — or grit my teeth and recite the prices, taking some pleasure in the obvious satisfaction it gives my Southeast Asian friends.)

Humans express themselves through non-verbal as well as verbal means. Westerners make more extensive use of facial expression and hand gestures than do most Southeast Asians. For example, my Cambodian friend once said that she understood her social worker's words but not what he meant. She explained in Cambodian to her daughter, imitating the elaborate hand gestures that the social worker and I had used unconsciously to make our points to one another. We might generalize by saying that Southeast Asians are more aware of their physical bearing and more controlled in their body movements than most Westerners. Our gestures openly express our emotions (we like to "let it all hang out"), whereas Southeast Asians seldom communicate in this manner. They generally carry themselves gracefully and maintain composure even when in contact with many people. Clumsy, uncoordinated movements are an embarrassment. Our vigorous gesturing, poking, touching, slapping on the back does not communicate friendship but it is an indication of our rudeness and lack of control over our bodies.

One important point concerns holding hands. It is not unusual for young women to walk together holding hands. It is equally common for young men to walk hand in hand or arm in arm. There is no implication of homosexuality in such normal behaviour, and it would be highly embarrassing if such an accusation were made. Refugees might want to know how Westerners are likely to interpret that behaviour, however. On the other hand, young men and women do not hold hands or show signs of affection in public. No doubt, this Western habit may be acquired quite quickly.

Young Western women who show casual interest in Southeast Asian males may find their friendliness misinterpreted. An eighteen-year-old Cambodian man attending a Western high school may be quite taken with the girls' dress and behaviour, which by Southeast Asian standards could be considered provocative. Casual friendship could be misinterpreted as sexual advance, to the embarrassment of both parties. On the other hand, Southeast Asian men may express fear that they will have no sexual life whatsoever since "Western women will think them too small and not be attracted to them."

It is useful to remember that women and girls from Southeast Asia may be more careful than North American women about keeping their bodies covered. A saleswoman who accompanies a young Loatian girl to the dressing-room may find the girl suddenly changes her mind about trying on a dress. A gym teacher who complains about a Vietnamese teenage girl refusing to take gym class may find that, to the teenager, the idea of dressing and undressing in a room with other girls is quite disturbing. A Cambodian woman may reject all skirts or dresses given to her by agencies or sponsors because they would leave her legs uncovered.

Widespread in Southeast Asia is the belief that the upper part of the body, particularly the head, should be regarded as sacred; and the feet, profane. Consequently, it is an insult to touch or tap another person on the head. A person's head must be treated with respect, and violating this principle could cause great misunderstanding. Conversely, the lower parts of the body, and particularly the feet, are correspondingly devalued. Pointing one's feet at someone's head is especially insulting. Often we sit with our legs up on a table with our feet pointing directly at another's head. While this is a comfortable, casual posture for us, it may cause great discomfort in a refugee and be interpreted as a deliberately insulting gesture.

Interpersonal Relations

It is difficult — even dangerous — to make generalizations about interpersonal relations. This approach easily slips into overgeneralizations and stereotyping. But the attempt must be made, for it is in the realm of interpersonal relations where most difficulties for refugees and sponsors lie.

Different cultures have different assumptions about how to interact with others on a day-to-day basis. These differences need not cause problems between sponsors and refugees. But some differences may indeed cause problems in certain contexts. The more we know about the refugees' experiences and their values, the better we will be able to comprehend the problems they face here. The comments that follow provide a background that may help sponsors understand how the refugees may interpret the new social situations they encounter.

Compared to Westerners, Southeast Asians generally present a much more polite, composed demeanour. In much face-to-face interaction, they may appear intent on searching for cues as to what we expect them to do or say. When we provide such cues, refugees will strive to give an answer or behave as they think we would want them to. In practical everyday terms, we may expect many Southeast Asians would avoid telling sponsors or friends anything that might distress them. Hence, many sponsors complain that they have no idea how the refugee family is *really* doing, or what they *really* need. Just as it would be impolite to say no when an affirmative answer is desired, so it might be impolite to say that one still does not understand what has just been explained — particularly if the speaker has taken pains to go over the point repeatedly.

Politeness is more than rules of etiquette imposed by one generation on a second. It is rather a "social cosmetic" that permits structuring behaviour to avoid offence. Polite evasions are responsible ways for individuals to avoid confrontation. This is not considered lying (which would break Buddhist precepts). It is simply part of a strategy for maintaining harmonious social relations.

Naturally, displays of anger, which disrupt social relations, would be considered rude. If at all possible, confrontation must be avoided, particularly with a patron or sponsor. If something unpleasant must be brought out into the open, it should be done indirectly to save face. If a sponsor gets angry at a refugee, for example, it is the sponsor who loses in the eyes of Southeast Asians. I once spoke sharply to a Laotian teenager who repeatedly ignored dental and tutoring appointments. The incident was passed on to his mother, who called her son over. I felt sure that she would tell him to come and apologize to me for his irresponsibility. Instead, he apologized for causing me to lose control of my temper.

There is an implication that follows from such emotional control. By controlling your own emotions, another person cannot easily figure out your intentions. In fact, there is an assumption that other people's motives and intentions cannot be easily known. This recognition of the indeterminacy of others' actions may be interpreted by Westerners as distrust. I would characterize the response of most of my Southeast Asian friends to a possible job or house, for example, as "I'll believe it when I see it." They seldom expressed disappointment when their expectations were not met, because there is a sense in which they might not have truly believed it in the first place. (Unlike my Cambodian friend, I am constantly expecting miracles — and being disappointed.)

We may respond that such emotional control and formality inhibits spontaneity and expression of real feelings and emotions. No one who has attended parties with Laotians, Cambodians, or Vietnamese could ever doubt their absolute delight in pleasant social occasions, their affability, and their capacity to participate openly and with great feeling in festive events.

Generous hospitality is not something special to Southeast Asians; it is automatic and considered the normal or natural thing to do regardless of economic circumstances. Offering drinks and meals to guests at appropriate times is taken for granted. Asking if a guest wants something to eat or drink might be considered impolite. A good host would simply bring refreshments. I recall a sponsor who continually asked the members of a refugee family if they would like a meal; she kept receiving a negative answer. Clearly, if their sponsor really meant the offer, food would appear automatically.

Another matter related to hospitality: sponsors may have noticed that Southeast Asians seldom make a fuss over wrapped gifts. They often put them aside to open privately. Westerners are used to elaborate expressions of excitement over wrapped presents, and they might mistake this custom for ingratitude. But the transfer from giver to receiver is essentially a private transaction — the giver knows what he has given and the receiver will soon know. Excessive thanks, when both parties know the nature of the reciprocal obligations, might appear gratuitous. If sponsors insist that the present be opened immediately, they may be nonplussed to find that they are immediately asked how much the present cost.

Teachers of Vietnamese children have often commented on the children's response to authority figures. In fact, stereotypes of Asians present them as docile, subservient, and willing to take orders. As with most stereotypes, this is a simplistic reduction of a much more complex set of values, including respect for age, respect for teachers, and a desire to know where a person fits in any set of clearly defined social relationships. Unstructured or ambiguous role definitions may cause anxiety for refugees. This anxiety arises from not knowing where others fit or where they themselves fit in a complex of fixed, stationary positions. A teacher who acts like a teacher provides cues for the student, who then acts like a student. A teacher who acts like a buddy leaves a refugee child wondering what behaviour is expected of him or her. Students may expect to be told what to memorize, and if any interpretation is necessary, it is the teacher's interpretation that is the authority. Our school systems have different expectations about the learning process, which refugee children may not easily understand.

Refugees can and will adapt in North American communities. Laotians, Cambodians, and Vietnamese are adaptable and resourceful people; they do not appear unwilling to accept some Western customs and institutions while retaining what is most valued in their respective cultural systems. They tolerate what we might consider ambiguity and are quite prepared to try a variety of solutions to problems. This pluralistic approach to problem solving allows for a gradual adjustment to North American communities, and the commmunities themselves will benefit from this bicultural adaptation.

Sponsorship

Refugees are trying to gain control over their lives. On their arrival, they have minimal power to redefine the situation to make life appear more meaningful or to increase their options. Gradually, they will gain this control over their own destinies. How well and how fast they gain this control depends partly on their sponsors.

Many people reading this book may be sponsors of Southeast Asian refugees, or they may be in a position to assist sponsors. What exactly is a sponsor? If the role were more clearly defined, or if there were readily available analogies for the role, many problems would disappear. In fact, there are no close analogies for interpreting the relation between a sponsor and a refugee. The Oxford dictionary defines a sponsor as someone who answers for someone else, someone who offers strong support, or someone who makes a formal promise or pledge on behalf of another. However the formal requirements of sponsorship may differ in diverse communities, sponsors should be prepared to absorb some of the culture shock that the refugees face in their first months in new communities. The sponsor is like a cultural broker — a person who mediates between cultural systems. Sponsors are the people who confront the refugees with the reality of living in a different culture. Living in the same house or nearby, they help the refugee negotiate the transition between two different ways of viewing the world. Although medical, dental, and educational problems may take a great deal of time, they are straightforward compared to problems of cultural adjustment. When a refugee family is perfectly comfortable with Westerners, easily able to recognize the subtle cues we are constantly giving about our social interaction, and able to manipulate our cultural rules for their own ends, then the responsibilities of sponsorship have ended.

Just as we could learn from Southeast Asians how to disengage ourselves from our children, how to desist from grasping, how to keep a "cool heart," so sponsors must accept that if they have done their job well, they must also let go, detach themselves from the refugees they have sponsored, and renegotiate a relationship based on friendship, common interests, and common experiences.[4]

---

4.   For suggested reading, see bibliography.

Vietnamese anniversary ceremony at Buddhist pagoda near Montreal.

11

Community and Inter-Ethnic Relations of Southeast Asian Refugees in Canada

by
Doreen Indra

Southeast Asian refugee communities in Canada are recent phenomena but already they are very complex social systems. This complexity has only now begun to be recognized by government, private agencies, and sponsors, and yet the forms that it takes will be crucial to Southeast Asian refugee orientations to Canada, Canadians, and to each other. A look at a few key organizational principles of community and social interaction among the Vietnamese, Sino-Vietnamese, Lao-speaking, and Cambodian people in Canada will help explain the complexity of the systems. The forms the community has taken in Edmonton, at least to the extent that this community is generally representative of community organization elsewhere, serve as the basis for these observations.

Ethnic Affiliation

Without any doubt, the most important organizing principle among Southeast Asian refugees is ethnic identity. Whereas the media, government, and sponsors may not have been much aware of it, refugees make very sharp distinctions between each other on the basis of ethnicity.[1] This is so much so that ethnic affiliation, or

---

1. For example, in Edmonton most social welfare workers and English as a second language teachers did not become aware for months that the majority of refugees in early 1979 were Chinese rather than Vietnamese. Even then, it took months more before the (false) revised thesis that they were "of Chinese origin but culturally Vietnamese" was rejected.

its lack, usually overrides objective criteria like the commonality of the refugee experience itself. With a few substantial exceptions, the Vietnamese, Vietnamese Chinese, Laotians, and Cambodians see each other as entirely distinct. Each forms what is for the most part an entirely separate community, based on its own criteria for membership, its own language, and its own customs. In these things, Southeast Asian refugees are no different than Europeans coming to Canada.

The Vietnamese have been here the longest, thus their community institutions are by far the most developed. Perhaps a thousand Vietnamese were living in Canada at the time of the American withdrawal from Vietnam in 1975. Most of these were students and professionals resident in metropolitan Montreal and Toronto. In both urban areas, Vietnamese formed their own associations as well as dense social networks linking one individual with another.

The downfall of the Thieu regime resulted in a second wave of four or five thousand Vietnamese immigrants in 1975-76. Most of these individuals were political refugees in the true sense of the word — army officers, middle-level bureaucrats, students, professionals, and skilled urban workers whose lives and livelihoods were directly threatened by the change in government. Violently anti-Communist and not a little anti-American, these individuals now make up most of the intellectual and organizational cores of Vietnamese communities across Canada.[2]

Although a number of Vietnamese continued to come to Canada after 1976, it was only in late 1978 that the flow increased again as people began the exodus out of Vietnam by sea. Perhaps 30 percent of Southeast Asian refugees who have arrived in Canada in the past two years (1978-79) have been Vietnamese. Greatly outnumbering those who came before them, these individuals are now representative of Vietnamese in Canada.

Vietnamese who were part of this third wave are of four basic types: (1) northern expatriates who left for the South when Ho Chi Minh took over in 1954; (2) middle-class individuals previously involved with the Thieu regime; (3) a wide variety of individuals who fled the South for primarily economic reasons; and (4) northerners. The educational, occupational, and class

---

2.   Their ambivalence towards the United States stems principally from their conviction that the United States let the South Vietnamese down.

backgrounds of third-wave immigrants were therefore far broader than those of Vietnamese who came earlier. Both ethnically and by other criteria, their identities are also considerably more varied.

Northerners and southerners, for instance, see themselves as experientially different. After the 1954 Geneva Agreement, over a million people migrated from the North to the South where they formed their own expatriate social networks. When, in 1975, the South was taken over by the North, these individuals were immediately at double risk: they had fled once and were therefore under suspicion by the new government. Pro-Communist southerners were equally suspicious of them because many northerners had moved into responsible positions in the South Vietnam government. Consequently, many fled Vietnam.

In Canada these double expatriates also form groups. Although they have been away from North Vietnam for twenty-five years, they strongly feel their identity as northerners. Northerners often see themselves as superior — as more authentically Vietnamese, less materialistic, more energetic, harder working, and clearer thinking than southerners.

The North-South split is even more marked between southerners and recent refugees from the North. Although both share Vietnamese language and basic Vietnamese cultural conventions, differences of history, political organization, social ideology, and war separate them. Paradoxically, although recent northerners fled Vietnam, they still profit ideologically from the fundamental winner-loser, North-South equation that the conclusion of the war produced. Northerners capitalize on the outcome, while southerners consider northerners to be tainted by communism.

Despite these (and many other) distinctions that Vietnamese make between themselves, their collective ethnic identity vis-à-vis non-Vietnamese is very, very strong. It is first of all an identity born out of conflict, initially with the Chinese, then the French, the Japanese, and the Americans. Vietnamese identity is intimately tied to the history of conquest and re-establishment of Vietnamese autonomy that surrounds this conflict (see Chi chapter 1).

Moreover, most Vietnamese refugees have known no other life than war; they have been born and raised in a society where catastrophe was an ever-present possibility. Planning for the future was always risky: any day they or their families could have been killed, their property destroyed, their livelihood eliminated.

Consequently, Vietnamese have evolved a very idealistic picture of what it means to be Vietnamese. They bring to Canada a deep sense of love of country and people.

Most importantly, their notion of Vietnamese includes only *ethnic* Vietnamese and specifically excludes all others who have been part of the Southeast Asian refugee flow — the Chinese, Laotians, and Cambodians in particular. Over many years of contact in Southeast Asia, strong prejudicial stereotypes for each group have developed, which effectively separates these groups socially once they arrive in Canada. To many Vietnamese, the Sino-Vietnamese are an untrustworthy, clannish, money-hungry, but admittedly hard-working people who cared little for Vietnam. As is frequently the case with rural peoples, the Lao are often stereotyped as lazy, dirty, unsophisticated, and meek. This sort of mutual stereotyping is, of course, a pervasive aspect of immigration from all parts of the world and is not particular to Southeast Asia.

In an analogous fashion, the Vietnamese Chinese have developed their own distinct sense of who they are, to the point where they too form quite autonomous communities here. Most ethnic Chinese in what was South Vietnam migrated there during the long period of European colonial rule. Most were originally from Guangdong and Fujian in southern China. Under the political and military umbrella of the French and the Americans, most of them were involved in one way or another in small business. Chauvinistic preference, and perhaps some rejection by the ethnic Vietnamese, led to the Chinese developing their own residential communities, each with its own parallel institutions — schools, shops, religious centres, and organizations. Over the years, Vietnamese Chinese slowly accepted a variety of Vietnamese cultural conventions while continuing to remain ethnically separate; slowly also they began to identify less and less with their region of origin in China.

Very few Chinese came to Canada from Vietnam before the fall of 1978. Hence, when they suddenly became the majority of Southeast Asian refugees, they had no community infrastructure developed anywhere in Canada. Those that have fled Vietnam have done so for a variety of reasons. Still, one factor cannot be ignored: Chinese see their exodus at least partially in ethnic relations terms. Whereas they see the "Communists" as being instrumental in denying them their traditional livelihood, they also see these

Communists as ethnic Vietnamese. Many Sino-Vietnamese refugees are (to say the least) very suspicious of ethnic Vietnamese refugees.[3] In addition, they too have their own less than flattering stereotype of the Vietnamese, who are often seen as untrustworthy, romantic, cruel, lazy spendthrifts. By contrast, many see themselves as rooted in thousands of years of Chinese tradition; they think of themselves as hard-working enterprising, clever, racially and culturally pure, and economically successful.

At the same time, large numbers of Sino-Vietnamese see themselves as quite distinct from other culturally Chinese groups in Canada, even though the majority share a common language (Cantonese) and basic cultural traditions. With few exceptions, Vietnamese Chinese do not, for instance, merge into social communities of Chinese Canadians from Hong Kong; part of this stems from a quite widespread feeling among some other Chinese communities that Vietnamese Chinese are backward, ill-educated, uncultured, poor, and unskilled.[4]

The overwhelming majority of Southeast Asian refugees who have arrived in Canada to date have been either Vietnamese or Sino-Vietnamese. Over the last year a small, slowly increasing number of Lao-speakers (hereafter called the Lao) have begun to arrive, chiefly as privately sponsored refugees. Most have been consciously sponsored by church organizations like the Mennonite Central Committee, which realized that these people were having a much harder time coming to Canada than others. By February, 1980, about a thousand Lao had arrived in Canada. They make up about 5 percent of the immigrant flow at present.

The Lao are from a very different cultural tradition than either the Vietnamese or the Sino-Vietnamese, with a distinctive language, religion, set of values and beliefs. Consequently, they too tend to form separate (albeit small) communities in Canada.[5] They are particularly suspicious of the Vietnamese, who have

---

3. Part of this suspicion is well founded. Without a doubt ethnic Vietnamese have had far greater input to government and the media than have the Chinese. A disproportionate number of interpreters and community workers funded by government are Vietnamese.

4. In addition, there is a widespread but never publicly voiced fear among many Chinese Canadians that the refugee influx may polarize other Canadians against them.

5. For instance, the present Lao population of Alberta (May, 1980) stands at about 200 individuals.

invaded their country and are perceived by the Lao as cruel, untrustworthy, sneaky but clever. The Lao dislike for the Vietnamese is a long-term part of the colonial legacy. As noted in other chapters, the French used Vietnamese to control Laos, and Lao middle- and upper-class people usually had to be educated in Vietnam where they often felt denigrated. The Vietnamese return the favour, frequently describing the Lao as lacking pride, as being unclean, uncultured, and lazy.

Despite the large number of Cambodians now in camps in Thailand, relatively few have come to Canada (with the exception of Quebec) and hence there are few Cambodian Canadian communities per se. However, Cambodians (and Lao) are an increasing proportion of refugees today. Suffice it to say that Cambodians will inevitably form another set of communities separate from the rest.

When these various people, identities, and mutual stereotypes are taken together, the consequence is that wherever "refugees" settle in Canada they will almost automatically attempt to follow their primary ethnic affiliation in developing their relations with others. In terms of material conditions in Canada and the refugee experience itself, all individuals may seem to be pretty much the same to Canadians. The point is that they are not the same, nor have they had a common history. The social fabric they subsequently weave will vary accordingly.

Family and Household

Many of the basic constraints of the settlement experience and the economy have so far generated a surprising degree of similarity in family and household organization among the Vietnamese and Sino-Vietnamese. Perhaps more than anything else, the lottery of fleeing Vietnam has been the most substantial leveller. The Vietnamese and Sino-Vietnamese come to Canada with broadly the same ideal model of family relations and household composition. Ideally, age is respected and family responsibility is carried by all. Ideally also, individuals should live together under one roof, forming a multi-person socio-economic unit that puts forward a united front to the challenges of the world. Vietnamese and Sino-Vietnamese families rarely conformed to the ideal, but extended family units — where elderly parents, some of their adult children, and their grandchildren lived together — were nonetheless common.

Few families have been fortunate enough to be able to recreate such a residence unit. Many escaped alone, leaving their families in Vietnam. Many others were less fortunate still and saw family members perish in the attempt. Still others are trying to find their relatives who have been distributed by fate to different refugee camps, receiving countries, provinces, and cities. Refugees must pick up the pieces and do what they can.

Individuals who have no close relatives here almost invariably get together in small groups segregated by ethnicity, age, and sex to set up temporary joint households — three young Chinese women here, five young Vietnamese men there. Within these households there is usually no overall authority, nor much in the way of formal rules. People generally share the rent and other costs and eat together. These households are understandably quite unstable and there is a constant flow of individuals among them. Still, these households are an important source of psychological security for new refugees, who are much in need of it. No new refugee need live alone if he or she does not wish to, at least in the major urban centres.

Beyond these households of single men or women, there are several other varieties that are centred around a married couple. These too have been primarily organized with an eye towards cutting individual costs, reducing loneliness and depression, and producing a semblance of roots. Kinship is also an important organizing principle. Indeed, kinship responsibilities frequently outweigh other factors, especially in the case of non-working relatives such as older people, youths, women with children, and those who are in English language classes or are retraining. In their best form, these "extended" households operate quite efficiently. The primary couple often exercises a degree of guidance and household authority not seen in households of single men or women. Frequently, a rather equitable division of household labour exists among men, with the universal qualification that women cook, clean, and care for children even if they also work full time.

In addition to these multicomponent households, an increasing number of Vietnamese and Sino-Vietnamese are living in nuclear family units. For some, this is the household form of choice, either because it signifies economic independence or because for some reason they wish to establish a less intense relationship with other community members. Because the economic costs of this option are high, this is typically a choice available only to the relatively well off. For others, there is no reasonable option. Some have such large families that living in an extended household is simply not practical. Other families have been moved into apartments by government or sponsors. Still others are without friends or relatives and are not outgoing enough to put forward the proposition of living with anyone else.

In overview, there is no typical form of refugee household arrangement, for there is a constant flow of personnel from one to another, with the consequence that household structure changes continuously. Despite this, there are key problems and processes at work within them. Much of the tension and trauma of the refugee experience is worked out in these contexts, and family organizations and values are now under rapid flux. For one thing, economic dictates have had profound effects on the relationship between the sexes and the generations. In Canada, many Vietnamese women and ethnic Chinese enter the public work force for the first time. Other women have taken on the added burden of being the family head. Typically, wives do not work in the same context as their husbands. While economically necessary, this often poses a direct challenge to the traditional (male) idea of family. Men in particular frequently suffer a loss of identity, for their stereotypic vision of themselves as breadwinners can no longer be maintained. At the same time, women's visions of the world are considerably expanded; no longer must they play only the roles of mother and wife (see Van Esterik, chapter 10). Husband-and-wife conflict frequently ensues.

Somewhat similar problems of role expectations and conflict over authority arise between the generations. Both Vietnamese and Sino-Vietnamese cultures stress respect for old people, especially family elders.[6] In Vietnam these traditional values were supported by everyday life; older people monopolized power and privilege and could therefore command respect, at least in their own social circles. Here, changes in family structure and the pressures on it have severely weakened parental authority and status. Children quickly orient towards their peers and consider their parents to be old-fashioned and overly traditional. Children frequently learn English more quickly than their parents and become linguistic and cultural middlemen between their parents and the rest of

6.   Both traditionally subscribe to Confucian standards, the Vietnamese more strongly than the Chinese.

the world. Children often correctly sense they know more about Canada than their parents, and often they do. Similar conflicts arise between adults and their elderly parents, as the latter often feel isolated, alone, powerless, and without respect. In all these things, Vietnamese and Sino-Vietnamese diverge little from other immigrant groups.

Although many of these familial stresses are heightened by the newness of settlement, they are certain to be chronic problems. Indeed, some of them are likely to grow as younger people become more and more acculturated. New social and economic conditions have produced a host of new responsibilities and demands on family members, and it is too recent for new codes of behaviour and belief to have arisen to deal with them. Value and behavioural ambiguity result.

The Social Organization of Communities

Neither Vietnamese, Chinese, nor Lao communities are residential communities.[7] Rather they are *social* communities — dense networks of overlapping social relations that tie one individual to another and collectively make something that is rather more than its constituent parts. However, neither type of ethnic social community is an amorphous whole. Inevitably, community *functions* to the benefit of some people rather than others. Inevitably also, individuals tend to associate primarily with others like themselves, and this leads to a complicated internal structure within each local community. These factors are somewhat different among Vietnamese than they are among Sino-Vietnamese; each set is discussed separately.

In an elementary sense, community social relations (and institutions) are considerably stronger, more frequent, and more important among Vietnamese than Chinese. This is the result of a number of things. First, Vietnamese as a group seem more damaged psychologically by leaving Vietnam. Most feel strongly that they are *political* refugees, who would immediately return to Vietnam if the political climate changed; many of them probably would. As such, they feel a loss of country that is at least as substantial as their loss of friends, relatives and economic position. Community partially compensates for this loss by providing an environment of Vietnamese culture and practice in a context

---

7.   There is often considerable residential clustering in low-rent areas, as well as near jobs and social services.

where everyone shares the same losses. Many Sino-Vietnamese apparently do not feel their loss of country nearly so strongly. Second, the Vietnamese sense of social welfare extends further than does that of the Chinese, at least in Canada. Most Vietnamese sense an obligation to help out other community members — and find it nearly impossible to deny assistance when it is requested. Among Vietnamese, informal systems of mutual aid arose congruently with initial settlement and are now quite strong. Individuals gain information, practical tips about jobs, training programs, social services, and occasionally financial assistance through community networks. Although Chinese individuals benefit from their community networks, these networks are not nearly so strong; for them family is the primary responsibility.[8] Third, Vietnamese communities have been established longer and consequently more individuals can be involved in interfamilial affairs than is the case with the Vietnamese Chinese. In most urban centres (where both groups have congregated), there have been Vietnamese for at least five years; in Toronto and Montreal, the comunities go back fifteen years. Virtually no Sino-Vietnamese community is more than two years old at present, and it is unrealistic to expect them to be well developed.

These differences also partially account for the unequal development of formal organizations among the Vietnamese and Sino-Vietnamese. Universally, Vietnamese associations are more likely to exist and are more forceful and organized than Sino-Vietnamese associations. For instance, the former have generated their own newsletters, recreational and community aid programs, and liaison with government and the media in ways not paralleled by the Chinese. This, in turn, has resulted in the Vietnamese effectively monopolizing public attention, even in places where they are a minority of refugees. In contrast, the Vietnamese Chinese consistently suffer a leadership and spokesperson vacuum.

In addition to these factors, this phenomenon is partially the result of demographic differences in the communities. Almost all Vietnamese communities have at least a small core of literate, educated, middle-class individuals, who migrate into leadership positions in formal organizations. Once there, their communication skills and knowledge about Western society are great assets. Sino-Vietnamese communities have almost nobody like this; formal

---

8.   Although less able to provide these functions due to their newness and small size, in these regards Lao communities follow the Vietnamese pattern.

organizations are hard to start and often ineffective. As a result, they have virtually no vehicles of their own through which to make their concerns known to government, press, and people.[9]

As mentioned, none of these communities is either homogeneous or free from conflict. Typically, the differences between one community member and another are sharp enough that it is difficult to say that any one person or point of view is representative. For instance, class divisions in Vietnamese communities are sharp enough that there is always the danger that the formal (middle-class) leadership's views do not reflect those of the communities at large. As a rule of thumb, Vietnamese leaders play down community problems, fearing that making them public would give the community a bad name. Informal Vietnamese social relations are also class stratified. Among the Chinese this is also the case, but the range of classes is not as great as with the Vietnamese.

Paralleling Vietnamese class distinctions is a fairly universal urban-rural dichotomy; even within the same socio-economic class, urban people are considered to be more civilized and to be of higher status. This is also true of the Chinese. Vietnamese also sort out along the threefold division between "pure" southerners, transplanted northerners, and those who have come directly from the North.

In addition, multiple stresses brought about by the traumatic refugee experience and subsequent settlement have made community social relations much more difficult than they would be otherwise. Both processes have altered the life chances of individuals in a dramatic and sometimes random fashion. In both communities, many individuals have suffered a great loss of power, privilege, and prestige. Well-off Vietnamese professionals and Chinese businessmen have been reduced to wage labourers; household heads have lost their families; the powerful have lost all power. Hence, previous relationships are frequently inverted; working-class Vietnamese serve as interpreters and, hence, as informal community spokespersons. Women work and young men frequently make more money than those in middle age. Both types of communities are therefore caught up in a massive redistribution of power, privilege, and prestige. This renegotiation is ongoing in every community and results in constantly shifting factions and political alliances.

---

9.   Lao people will probably follow the Vietnamese pattern to the extent that they have literate spokespersons among them.

It is also seriously undermining traditional values. Younger Vietnamese are increasingly seeing the demise of Vietnam as a series of failures guided by older men, and this contradicts the ideal of respect for elders. Similarly, if Vietnamese here were, for instance, to visualize the ideal leader of an association, it would be an educated, well-off, married older man; unfortunately, the most dynamic and forceful potential leaders are often recognized to be younger men, whose language and other communications skills are better.

A similar erosion is occurring in how both Vietnamese and, secondarily, Chinese view the basis of behaviour. Vietnamese in particular have tended to view the world in moralistic terms; there are good and bad people out of which flow good and bad respectively. In this regard one need only point to Ho Chi Minh; by contrast, an expedient leader like Mao would not fit the ideal. Here in North America, pragmatism has recognized advantages and frequently contradicts this dualistic universe. Refugees must work with, live with, and seek help from individuals whom they view as morally questionable. Indeed, their whole value system is afloat, and the detachment this brings is often confusing. For many, there is no clear moral path, no set of values that do not seem a little arbitrary.

One final comment on community organization is in order. Neither Sino-Vietnamese nor most Vietnamese have as yet developed an extensive range of parallel institutions. However, communities across Canada have already organized to celebrate the Vietnamese, Chinese, and Lao new year. Vietnamese and a few Chinese newsletters have been started, and formal organizations will inevitably be formed everywhere there are more than a few hundred individuals from either community. In larger centres like Montreal, Toronto, and Vancouver, Vietnamese have already begun to establish a limited number of businesses catering at least in part to other Vietnamese, especially restaurants and food stores. Sino-Vietnamese businessmen are likely to soon follow; they are now limited only by the lack of capital.

Social Interaction with Others

Refugee interaction with others can be separated into two types: interaction with refugees from other ethnic backgrounds, and interaction with "Canadians" (everybody else). At this point these are quite different, for they are based on different presuppositions and accomplish different functions.

Whereas Vietnamese and Sino-Vietnamese form distinct ethnic communities, there is, nevertheless, considerable interaction between some individuals. If nothing else, the refugee experience guarantees this. They share that experience, and especially for the young this common denominator creates a strong bond; in any case, younger Sino-Vietnamese know Vietnamese and share a number of Vietnamese values. These individuals move rather easily between groups in Canada, perhaps in part because they are no longer constrained by parents and social situation to remain distinct.

Technical and procedural aspects of settlement also bring them together. Vietnamese and Sino-Vietnamese meet in English as a second language and other classes and in the context of government and private service agencies. Both also meet frequently in the work place. These functional encounters, however, are rarely sufficient to create long-term bonds.

A final connection between Vietnamese and Sino-Vietnamese stems from intermarriage. In Vietnam a considerable number of Chinese men married ethnic Vietnamese women; in the past the latter individuals were incorporated into the Chinese community.[10] Nonetheless, these marrriages have created intergroup social ties and have lowered intergroup cultural differences.

Relations between refugees and others are complex and difficult to summarize, for they depend much on individual and situation. Consequently, Vietnamese and Chinese orientations to Canadians warrant touching on briefly, as do points relating to refugee relations with sponsors, aid agencies, and others.

There are a number of rather substantial differences between the way Vietnamese and Sino-Vietnamese view their relationship to Canada and Canadians. Neither understand Canada very well at this point, but both groups are trying to, each in terms of its own values and expectations. It would be fair to say, on the basis of my observations, that Vietnamese generally seek to understand Canada in a more wide-ranging and philosophical sense than do the Chinese. Like the Chinese, they want to know about things that will help them materially, but they are also interested in what

---

10. Marriages between Vietnamese men and Chinese women sometimes occur but have traditionally been frowned upon by the Chinese.

Canada has to offer in the way of enjoyment, travel, culture, politics, and ideas; they are not afraid to sample any of these. In contrast, the newly arrived Chinese seem much more culturally conservative. Their adventures into the realm of Canadian society have so far been chiefly functional, involved in work, expenditure, and education. What partially compensates for this trend is the fact that the Chinese have an immigrant tradition and were already ideologically separate from Vietnam.

These differences are already evident in how children from these communities interact with their peers; this, in turn, is a function of their parents' differing cultural expectations. Based on the indications so far, Vietnamese children orient more strongly to their Canadian peers and are far less likely to maintain their traditional culture and language than are their Chinese classmates.

Relations with sponsors are frequently the most important intergroup ties that refugees have. It is fair to say that the sponsorship program borders on the incredible: rarely does so much good come out of a situation where the individuals involved understand each other so little. For their part, incoming refugees know virtually nothing about the concept of sponsorship — what a sponsor is, what a sponsor's responsibilities are, why someone would be a sponsor anyway. Typically, they are seldom told these things in a formal context, although some aid organizations are now holding orientation sessions in order to try to fill this informational vacuum. Most refugees, however, find out about sponsorship virtually through osmosis. Sponsors are usually no better informed about refugees than refugees are about them. This mutual ignorance is compounded by cultural difference and by the inability of sponsors and refugees to communicate easily with each other. It is all very confusing.

From the refugees' point of view, sponsorship is at once rewarding and extremely frustrating. Refugees are well aware that they are being assisted in settlement in some very substantial ways. They are grateful but often do not know how to respond. Traditional values demand that they reciprocate, but how can they? On the other hand, etiquette and communication difficulties frequently do not allow refugees to voice objections or qualifications to what sponsors do for them. Examples of this are legion. A common complaint is that sponsors find jobs for refugees (a good thing) where there are no other refugees (a bad thing); dare a refugee complain? Another frequent objection is that sponsors virtually smother refugees — they overassist them and allow them little privacy or control over their destinies. This indirectly attacks refugee confidence and self-respect, both of which are likely to be at a low ebb already.

Sponsor inexperience also occasionally creates problems of an ethnic or interpersonal nature. For instance, a sponsor group may at times be sponsoring three or four adults who are of different ethnic backgrounds, without realizing fully the problems this raises. Occasionally, the "families" sponsored by others are not families at all, and this is almost never realized.[11]

Refugees bewilderment produces its share of problems, too. Unaware of the limits of the sponsorship role, they frequently appear overdemanding or inconsistent. Likewise, they rarely have any idea of the degree to which sponsors are (or are not) suffering inconvenience of a financial burden as a result of sponsorship.

Relations with government and private settlement agencies follow a similar path. For their part, government and agency personnel who work frequently with refugees are often not fully aware of the situation, culture, history, needs, or goals of refugees, yet many believe they are. Their information on what refugees are about is often so limited and self-consistent that some believe they understand more than they do. Many of these service personnel have had to operate under extreme pressure and are constantly overworked. This, rather than their depth of knowledge, is the primary constraint. On the other side, refugees do not understand the Canadian social welfare system. They do not know what is their due and consequently do not fully benefit from the services available, or over-utilize them; in overview, they tend towards under-utilization.

These difficulties seem to be most prevalent in three areas of government-refugee interaction: immigration and settlement services, employment services and counselling, and English as a second language courses.

It should be noted that other sorts of interaction between refugees and Canadians are expanding rapidly. Refugees are developing Canadian friends and some are establishing links with a variety of Canadian churches.[12] Contacts with other workers are

---

11. Refugees in the camps believe that the Canadian government prefers to accept families, and so they team up to create fictitious family units.

12. The virtual absence of Buddhist religious institutions is something of a problem for both groups.

also becoming more important. In addition, some Sino-Vietnamese are establishing relationships with Chinese individuals from other places, though these relationships are much less frequent than those with other Sino-Vietnamese. Nevertheless, the contributions of non-Vietnamese Chinese have been helpful in assisting with refugee settlement.

Refugee Social Organization: An Overview

At this point refugee social organization is changing rapidly, as one would expect of immigrants who have come so recently and who have had to deal with so much. In order to make any sense out of the situation at all, I have concentrated here upon evident structures and processes and in so doing have certainly generated what is an overly ordered picture of the social phenomenon involved. No study as short as this can address properly what are equally vital parts of the settlement process so far — the ambiguity, the chaos and disorganization, the conflict, fear, sorrow and joy. Neither can it convey adequately the range of personal and situational variation involved in virtually everything mentioned here.

Still, it is fair to say that across the country there are strong trends towards order and consistency developing at the levels of self-identity, family, and community that reflect the ideas presented here. All in all, Southeast Asian refugees have shown themselves to be efficient and innovative social engineers, and they are to be credited for their substantial adaptability in developing their new social and ideological universe. Despite difficulties, the contributions of government, private agencies, sponsors, and other Canadians to this process have been very real and deserve recognition.

Nevertheless, the considerable progress so far in refugee settlement should delude none into thinking that concomitant social problems arising out of the exodus are going to disappear overnight. They will not. Rather, as refugees become more settled, their social problems will shift in kind more than in quantity. Now, they are short-term and concrete. In the future they are likely to be more subtle and developmental. Even if Southeast Asian immigration were to end today, those who are here will be working out its consequences for a long time.[13]

---

13.   In this, I believe that private settlement agencies will play an increasing role, chiefly as facilitators and as liaisons between Southeast Asian immigrants and the larger society.

Young Cambodian child queueing for food at Sakaeo, Thailand.

MR.
GOUDAS

PATNA
LONG GRAIN
RICE

Vietnamese refugee at work in Montreal.

12

The Economic Adaptation of Southeast Asian Refugees in Canada

by
Norman Buchignani

Once they have arrived in Canada, Southeast Asian refugees are faced with the prospect of establishing an economic foundation for themselves and their families. Minimally, they must develop an adequate income and must find ways to convert that income effectively into what they need to make a go of it here. Inasmuch as Southeast Asian refugees exert a negligible influence upon the Canadian economy, this process is viewed primarily as one of economic adaptation to the constraints of the economy as it exists at present.[1]

Clearly, there is no single type of Southeast Asian refugee. Individuals come from a wide range of class, occupational, educational, familial, and experiential backgrounds. Neither are the socio-economic contexts into which they come the same; Halifax job prospects, for example, are not what they are in Edmonton. Consequently, one can expect refugees do not have a single place in the Canadian economy, nor do they express a simple adaptation to it. Already there is a wide variation in both.

Common Constraints

At the same time, several important economic constraints have generated a number of broad consistencies in how refugees

---

1. Accommodative changes in the Canadian economy in response to Southeast Asian refugees have been negligible.

have interacted with the economy, especially among those who have arrived since the beginning of 1979. Perhaps the most important of these is the refugee experience itself. Those Vietnamese who left in the chaos of the American withdrawal from South Vietnam in 1975 inevitably fled with only a few personal belongings. Few could have foreseen how quickly the Thieu regime would disintegrate, and hence few, except the élite, attempted to consolidate economic assets into a transportable, liquid form. The only economic resources that most were able to bring with them were their considerable occupational, education, and linguistic skills.

This contraint has operated even more severely on those who have fled since 1978. Most of these people had to escape covertly, and hence attempted to bring their savings with them. Nevertheless, because of meagre initial savings, the cost of buying oneself out of the country, and routine expropriation of their savings on the high seas or in the camps, very few have been able to bring with them more than a few thousand dollars. Most bring with them no funds whatsoever. In short, this constraint dictates that wage or salaried labour will be almost everyone's initial way of earning a living.

Moreover, few recent refugees have come to Canada with their family-based economic units intact. Wives, husbands, parents, brothers, sisters, and children, who together might have formed a mutually supporting economic entity in Vietnam, Cambodia, and Laos, have frequently been separated by the exodus. Whereas there, a common economic strategy was for a family to pool a number of incomes, which could be by themselves erratic or marginal, this option is far less available here.

Once in Canada, another common constraint comes into play. For several reasons the great majority of those who can work do so, even if this means taking extremely marginal jobs. This is the expectation of government and many sponsors, at least at a practical level. Policy statements aside, federal agencies typically have seen their responsibility for refugee settlement quite narrowly; financial support is usually forthcoming for basic necessities only until a refugee has found housing and employment. Thereafter, government responsibility ends. This "support them until they get a job" mentality has resulted in refugee adults being methodically fed into the job market as soon as they arrive in Canada. Although virtually all adult refugees express a strong desire to take English

TABLE 1

Intended Occupation of Adult Immigrants
from South Vietnam (1976)[2]

Intended Occupation	Number	Percentage of Adult Immigrants
Managerial	59	3.69
Sciences	98	6.13
Teaching	43	2.69
Medicine	105	6.56
Performing arts	14	0.88
Clerical	98	6.13
Sales	33	2.06
Service	30	1.88
Fabrication	50	3.13
Construction	17	1.06
Transportation	26	1.63
Other	146	9.63
Total	*721*	*45.06*
Non-working spouses	256	16.00
Students (over 18 years)	562	35.13
Other non-working	61	3.81
Total	*879*	*54.94*
Grand total	*1,600*	*100.00*

or French language classes, many apparently lack enough financial support from the government to enable them to attend or to complete these classes before they go out to work.[3] The major exception to this tendency is in Quebec.

Sponsors quite frequently hold the same view of what economically constitutes a successful settlement; I need only point

2. Employment and Immigration Canada, *1976 Immigration Statistics*, (Manpower and Immigration), 1977, pp. 36–49.

3. A 1978 survey of Vietnamese in Edmonton showed that 64 percent of respondents saw English language training as a necessary requisite to their employment upgrading (Canada Employment Centre, Edmonton, *Report of the Viets in Edmonton*, 1978, p. 7). By their own assessment, only 5 percent of adult refugees who arrived in Alberta during 1979 have adequate English.

to a first-hand encounter with a well-meaning sponsor who was inquiring about the progress of the doctor he had sponsored. The doctor had been here a month and in English as a second language classes for only two weeks. The sponsor had found the doctor a job in a local hospital and wanted to take him out of the ESL classes. The job was in the hospital kitchen. For skilled refugees, quick entry into marginal jobs can result in an occupational mobility trap.

This strong pressure by sponsors and government for refugees to enter the work force quickly cannot, however, be seen as an unambiguously bad thing. It depends on whom one is talking about. Many refugees are actually eager to get a job as soon as possible, and there are several good reasons for doing so. Many voice the same objections to being supported by sponsors or the government that one might expect from a North American: they dislike being economically dependent and consider it immoral, self-denigrating, or a nasty necessity to be eliminated as soon as possible. At the same time, the refugee experience has imbued in most a quality that immigrants share generally — the ability to view very pragmatically the short-term economic horizon. Consequently, refugees generally have few reservations against seeking work in occupations that in Southeast Asia would have been unthinkable on status and self-identity grounds. For all but a few, home-country occupational status calculuses have been temporarily shelved while people get themselves on their feet in whatever way they can. As a general rule, skilled refugees generally accept jobs at first which are far below their previous occupations. It should be noted that occupational status inconsistency of this sort is likely to be a severe problem in the future, when many refugees realize that their present occupational statuses are likely to be more or less permanent (see Van Esterik, chapter 10).

Further pressure to enter the job market quickly comes from strictly economic considerations. Refugees must eat, and therefore they must work; they have no other option. Moreover, virtually every adult individual expects to be able to support the immigration of relatives who are in their home country or in one of the Southeast Asian refugee camps. In order to be able to do this, refugees must demonstrate that they have the financial means to support their relatives. This has led to a number of individuals taking on two low-paying jobs in order to have the requisite level of income.

The new wave of refugees from Vietnam, which began in 1978, does not compare favourably on skill and educational criteria with those who came earlier. For example, the families of many of the Vietnamese Chinese who escaped over the past few years have been engaged in small-scale entrepreneurship: operating small food stores, engaging in manufacturing operations, wholesaling, sewing, and so forth. Vietnamese Chinese children and women were frequently drafted into the family business at an early age and hence received little education or formal occupational training. The same would hold for many Vietnamese as well, who tend to be less skilled than their 1975-76 compatriots. It is even more true of Cambodians and Laotians, most of whom have had very little experience with modern economic systems. Statistics for Southeast Asian refugees arriving in Alberta during 1979 (3,050 individuals) show that 30.4 percent of adults have completed primary school or less; only 22.05 percent have completed high school or more.[4] The average adult has about eight years of formal education. Individuals who are unskilled by Canadian standards tend to seek work quickly, for there are few alternatives.

Finding a Job

In a country with one million unemployed, finding work is not automatic for anyone, and it is by no means so for refugees. Although there is little quantitative data yet available for the country as a whole, there do seem to be several trends developing. First, skilled workers and professionals (mostly ethnic Vietnamese) seem to have experienced a sharp drop in occupational status. Beyond the newness of their situation, several factors account for this trend: lack of English or French fluency, lack of supporting documentation necessary for recertification, and the contradiction between the necessity of earning a living and the need to retrain. It is not at all uncommon to see highly trained refugees working in factories and restaurants and at manual labour. As a rule, two classes of skilled workers seem to be especially downwardly mobile — those in "humanistic" professions like teaching and the social sciences, and those whose skills have no precise equivalent here.[5] In contrast, those in medicine, the "hard"

4. Alberta Advanced Education and Manpower, "Report on the Movement of Indochinese Refugees to Alberta in 1979," mimeographed, 1980, pp. 9-11, 21.

5. Nguyen Quy Bong, "The Vietnamese in Canada: Some Settlement Problems," in V. Ujimoto and G. Hirabayashi, eds., *Visible Minorities in Canada* (Scarborough: Butterworths, 1980), pp. 247-56.

sciences, and engineering have a considerably easier time returning to their occupations — at least in being recertified.

At the same time, many individuals have entered the work
force who were never formally in it in Vietnam, particularly
women and young men. In places like Edmonton where work is
relatively easily available, virtually all young men who were
students or were unemployed in Vietnam are currently working;
so also are the majority of adult women. In other parts of the
country, these same people are actively seeking work, but poorer
economic conditions make it considerably more difficult for them
to be successful. This has produced enormous frustration among
these refugees.

For the majority, the situation is rather ambiguous and
unclear at present. The average occupational level of recent
immigrants is quite low, even by the estimation of the refugees
themselves, and this makes it difficult to evaluate their success
in adapting to the Canadian economy.

Economic conditions in their part of Canada have a crucial
effect on the economic life chances of these individuals. Willingness
to work is generally given, but available jobs are not. Whereas in
Alberta most of these individuals have obtained some sort of full-
time work, this is not the case elsewhere. In fact, economic
prospects in the East for individuals with limited skills have been
poor enough that a substantial migration pattern of Vietnamese
and Vietnamese Chinese to Alberta is already well established.
The potential exists in eastern Canadian urban contexts for the
formation of a relatively permanent economic underclass of
Vietnamese and Chinese refugees. On the other hand, refugees
have made extensive use of community networks to find out about
job openings. This source of information often allows individuals
to secure jobs before they are formally advertised and somewhat
compensates for lack of experience and skills.

On the Job

Refugees typically face many initial difficulties on the job.
These are of three basic type: (1) those stemming from intercultural
differences; (2) those from communication difficulties; and (3) those
that derive from novel aspects of the work environment.

TABLE 2

Occupational Groups of Adult Southeast Asian Refugees
(arrival in Canada January 1, 1979, to January 19, 1980)[6]

Stated Previous Occupation	*Number*	*Percentage of Adult Immigrants*
Managerial	66	0.55
Science	233	1.93
Teaching	288	2.38
Performing	150	1.24
Clerical	780	6.46
Sales	294	2.43
Services	463	3.83
Farming, fishing	266	2.20
Processing	492	4.09
Machining	343	2.84
Fabrication	3,376	27.94
Construction	519	4.30
Other occupations	1,264	10.46
Total	*8,474*	*70.14*
Non-working spouses	2,810	23.26
Students (over 18 years)	419	3.47
Other non-working	378	3.13
Total	*3,607*	*29.86*
Grand total	*12,081*	*100.00*

Despite a long history of European colonialism, Vietnamese, Vietnamese Chinese, Laotian, and Cambodian cultural conventions are quite different from Canadian ones, and some of these differences make for problems at work. Perhaps the most common of these is a different model of work and employer-employee relations. Work in Southeast Asia is characteristically placed in a larger context of patron-client relations.[7] There, an employee acknowledges the superior power and status of his employer and in return

---

6.   Employment and Immigration Canada.

7.   Tan Minh Tung, "Perspectives: Vietnamese Views on Resettlement and Adjustment," mimeographed (New York: 87th Annual Convention of the American Psychological Association, 1979).

receives paternalistic protection; as an ideal type, it is almost like a stern father-son relationship. A basic outgrowth of this sort of relationship is a much more integrative and long-term assessment of an individual's performance as an employee. Just as a father tolerates small-scale indiscretions on the part of his son, the employer in Vietnam typically gives an employee far more latitude than his Canadian counterpart in coming to work on time, appearing every day, and the like. The compensation for the employer is autocratic, unquestioned power on the job.

These types of relationships in the work place are rare in Canada. Consequently, new refugees frequently (and unknowingly) come into conflict with the expectations of their Canadian employers. Initially, they are very casual about arriving for work on time — one expression of the notorious use of a "rubber watch." Once more, Laotians and Cambodians seem to exhibit this tendency more than others. Similarly, refugees frequently consider that a wide variety of personal demands are sufficient reasons for not showing up for work at all.

In a more general sense, the absence of any sort of patron-client relationship between themselves and their Canadian bosses frequently compounds the alienation and lack of commitment with their present jobs that most refugees would feel in any case. Southeast Asian workers sense that status and rank in the work place are fuzzy and unclear and are constantly frustrated that their employers and fellow workers do not really know who they are.

A somewhat different perspective on work also arises among refugees who come from what was previously North Vietnam. Refugees from the North are profoundly alienated from the government there, and this alienation spills over on to their relationship to work. There, work is something required by the government — something to be endured for the extrinsic benefits that it brings. Some northern refugees have a difficult time adjusting to a "free" labour market. Again, Cambodians and Laotians have an even more difficult time. Those who have been in the camps for years may be cynical, suspicious, and disoriented.

Most on-the-job communication difficulties stem from lack of English or French fluency, though some of them are cultural in origin. Lack of effective English and French fluency among new immigrants is in excess of 90 percent. This greatly affects the type of job for which an employer will hire a refugee. In the manufacturing and processing sector, employers have rather consistently hired monolingual refugees into two types of jobs: those where refugee Vietnamese and Vietnamese Chinese workers can be organized into groups, each with an individual who can speak English, or those jobs that are extremely routine. Conversely, many employers will not hire refugees without English when the job in question requires custom work or moving from one job station to another. There also is a tendency to keep refugees away from situations where linguistic inability might lead to more industrial accidents. It goes almost without saying that no refugee who possesses a skilled occupation has much of a chance at working in his or her field without knowledge of the locally prevailing national language. Language facility is crucial.

Cultural considerations also impede communication on the job. Refugee employees know little about either the social etiquette of the job or their rights on it. Refugees are enough concerned about "face" that they are reluctant to ask for information from management or other workers. In addition, they rarely activate their work place rights, not realizing that these rights are far more substantial than they were in Vietnam, Laos, or Cambodia. As a consequence, there are many instances where refugees do not report industrial accidents, or they work below the minimum wage, on grossly extended shifts, or under unsafe conditions.

Income

Marginal jobs mean marginal incomes. In the light of the occupational constraints noted above, it should be no surprise that post-1977 refugees make very little money — typically earning less than $5 an hour and less than $8,000 a year (net) as full-time workers. While data on 1975-76 refugees in the United States suggest that individual workers there were able to improve their incomes substantially in the first two years, these relatively better-educated refugees still made less than $200 a week after two years in North America.[8]

In the Canadian context, this means that refugee families are consigned to temporary poverty if they are supported by only one wage earner. Refugees know this full well and have responded to the problem in two ways. First, they try to increase their individual

---

8.   Darrell Montero, "Vietnamese Refugees in America: Toward a Theory of Spontaneous International Migration," *International Migration Review* 8 (1979):624–48.

incomes by moving from job to job, even if the better-paying job offers less in the way of long-term prospects for advancement. Alternatively, they sometimes take on two jobs at the same time. Second, those whose families are here try to compensate for one low-paying job by securing another (low-paying) job for another family member. Although two marginal jobs frequently still do not bring refugee families up to the income level of the average Canadian family, it makes all the difference in terms of the concrete standard of living of the refugee family.

It should be noted that all refugees normally have access to another short-term source of income — sponsor or governmental support. It is fair to say that private sponsor support is so much more substantial than that provided by the government that in the short term it has resulted in an almost class-like difference between the life chances of privately and governmentally sponsored individuals. Private sponsorship frequently provides better housing, clothing, "start money," job prospects, and language training than does government sponsorship. This leads in turn to enhanced ability to afford the luxury of language training. Privately sponsored individuals therefore tend to be better off financially when they begin to work than are their government-sponsored compatriots.

Expenditures

Whereas refugees seem to have adapted in very similar ways to work, parallels between the communities seem to be somewhat weaker when one looks at how money is spent. If Vietnamese and Chinese Vietnamese are compared, individuals from both groups have fairly low individual incomes and have developed a number of similar strategies to reduce expenditures. One of the most prevalent is to lower costs by living together with members of their community. Most recent refugees who have come here without their families reside at present with other refugees. Typically, two to four individuals will band together to share what would otherwise be burdensome costs for rent, utilities, and furniture. Another alternative is for individuals to come to a similar arrangement with households that have a family or families at their centres. In the latter case, wide-ranging kinship systems and chain migration frequently generate households that are quite large by Canadian standards. In either case, this strategy has allowed refugees to enjoy a standard of living that is much better than might have been predicted from their low incomes. While these households are not true joint households in an economic sense, the individuals involved do benefit from the economy of scale, and living in them often has many more intangible economic benefits: some of these include access to information about jobs and training programs, the use of household mates for small loans, and the maintenance of a good psychological state.

More generally, both Vietnamese and Vietnamese Chinese have found it difficult to develop much in the way of savings. Regardless of their household organization, individuals have had to outlay what is for them a lot of money for rental deposits, car down payments, furniture, and insurance. Most are therefore in debt. Although most individuals in both groups tend to try very hard to save, few have been able to accumulate enough money for a down payment on a house.

The initial costs involved in settlement are not the only reasons for this. In addition, many refugees are caught between the cultural desire to save and their obligations to others. Virtually all refugees from Vietnam spend a substantial part of their earnings on goods and cash which they send to relatives in Vietnam or in the refugee camps; for most, this obligation is so strong that it borders on the necessary. Medicine and food products not available in Vietnam stream in from relatives here, while others remit large sums of money they hope will allow their relatives to escape. These contradictory demands continually place individuals in a dilemma. On one hand, the suffering of their Vietnam relatives is very real. On the other, every remittance lessens the life chances of those who are here. Refugees typically see their hard work result in a slow accumulation of funds, only to watch their savings disappear in this fashion. On top of this, Vietnamese in particular face the same dilemma here; honour and status considerations frequently demand that one offer assistance to fellow refugees in need, regardless of the consequences. In these regards, refugees are caught up between two rather different economic systems — our "free market" system and an older, paternalistic, kin-based system where interpersonal duties and obligations played an important role.

General similarities aside, there are a few differences in ethnic Vietnamese and Vietnamese Chinese economic adaptations to Canada. (About the Lao and Cambodians it is still impossible to say.) Broadly speaking, Vietnamese and Vietnamese Chinese see themselves as very different types of refugee: the former universally claim to be *political* refugees, while many Chinese see themselves as *economic* refugees. This marked difference is reflected in economic activity here. Vietnamese tend to be considerably less future-sighted than do the Chinese, at least with respect to how they spend their money. Vietnamese have rapidly accepted Canadian "buy now, pay later" patterns of expenditures and, when they can afford it, disdain used cars, furniture, and old housing. Being political refugees, they tend to be caught up in the moment, very much saddened by their loss of country, and distracted by social concerns from concentrating totally on the economic future. In contrast, the Vietnamese Chinese have been much more future-oriented, albeit in a very traditional way. It is the young Chinese who mainly miss Vietnam in the way that the ethnic Vietnamese do, and hence the rest have quickly settled down to consolidate their economic positions here. Families especially try as best they can to minimize expenditure on consumer goods and to save money. Although the Chinese also face the necessity of helping their relatives, they do frequently find a way to save. As one Vietnamese put it at a lavish Vietnamese New Year's celebration, "Today, we Vietnamese celebrate in this fine hotel. Tomorrow the Chinese will own it." This conclusion is much overdrawn, but many Chinese do have an eye on the possibility of returning to entrepreneurial occupations; virtually none have yet done so.

In overview, the present material standard of living of Southeast Asian refugees can be looked at in two ways. Relative to other Canadians they are disadvantaged. Refugees feel this, as well as an enormous sense of frustration and self-sacrifice. Particularly among the skilled, educated, and business classes there is considerable resentment and confusion over their status loss as well as the occasional loss of a better material standard of living. At the same time, many refugees have experienced a dramatic increase in their material living conditions. Owning a car in Vietnam was an élite privilege and it was unheard of in Laos, while here it is commonplace; there an urban worker might live in accommodations no bigger than a suburban Canadian living-room; access to education and social services were severely restricted. Many refugees are pleased with what they have already accomplished here economically, and this somewhat compensates for the enormous social and psychological losses produced by leaving their homeland.

Future Prospects

In consideration of the points raised here, the short-term economic prospects of Southeast Asian refugees are ambiguous. On the one hand, individuals from both groups have quickly adapted to the basic constraints of the Canadian economy. If the economic adaptation of 1975-76 Vietnamese refugees in the United States is even roughly similar, within two years of arrival virtually all refugee households will be self-supporting and the need for continuing governmental assistance will be low.[9]

At the same time, this minimal economic adaptation will not be sufficient for an increasing number of individuals. Dissatisfied with their economic lot, many will be then moving to the second stage of adaptation — into the slow process of upgrading, retraining, or recertification. However, this will likely be the path over which only a minority will be able to pass. Similarly, large-scale unemployment and underemployment will likely persist for a long time, just as lack of fluency in English or French will continue to limit job mobility.

In the longer term, one can expect that the economic class distribution of refugees will broaden enormously as those with superior education and skills consolidate their positions. One of the consequences of this will almost certainly be a further domination of community leadership position by the economically well-off. Whereas this is neither good nor bad per se, it is likely to pose one predictable difficulty for refugee economic adaptation that may be seen in other immigrant communities with similar leadership — the tendency of the leadership to publicly downplay the importance of economic problems within the community to the point where it interferes with the development of programs addressed to middle-range economic adjustment.

Indeed, it is towards middle-range programs aimed at upgrading and recertification that future efforts should be directed; at present there seems to be an imminent danger that such programs will never get off the ground. Unless government policy makes a substantial turnabout, the large-scale Southeast Asian refugee program is now virtually at its end. Southeast Asian immigration subsequent to 1980 is therefore likely to derive primarily from normal immigration channels. As such, an increasing number of Southeast Asian immigrants will not be

---

9.   *Ibid.*

formal refugees. In concrete terms this means that they will not have access to the short-term economic assistance that formal refugee status grants. Consequently, the initial economic base of post-1980 immigrants is likely to be at least as tenuous as that of refugees today. Many will be able to depend on the assistance of relatives during the settlement process, but this will be at least partially negated by the lack of benefits forthcoming to formal refugees. Economic costs now borne by private sponsors and government will be in essence transferred over to community members.

As the refugee flow slackens and the "boat people" vanish from the front pages of the newspapers, there is a likelihood that many of the special assistance programs that have arisen to assist Southeast Asian refugees will die. If this occurs, if refugees are left entirely to their own devices to better themselves economically, the costs are likely to be very high. As in other areas of life, economic adaptation to a new environment is not a thing that can be accomplished in a matter of months. At this point refugees are firmly in the economy, but they have by no means maximally adapted to it. The presence or absence of programs and agencies with a charter to assist these new Canadians in the coming years is therefore certain to have a substantial effect on the eventual role these individuals will have in the Canadian economy. This, in turn, will be of great consequence in determining the *long-term* place of Southeast Asians in Canadian society.

UNHCR/H. Gloaguen

Vietnamese anniversary ceremony at Buddhist pagoda near Montreal.

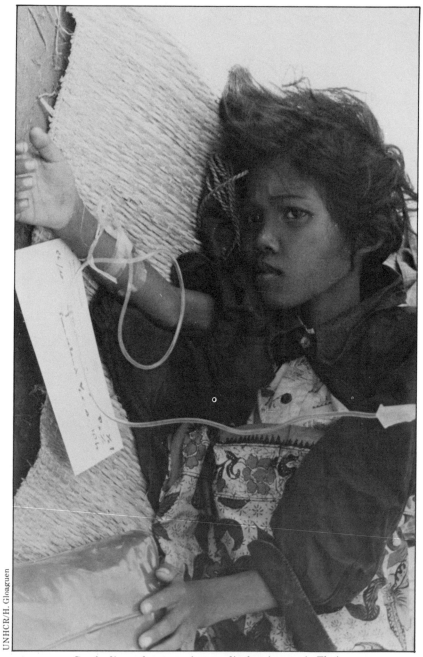

Cambodian refugee receives medical assistance in Thai camp.

13

Psychiatric Problems of Immigrants and Refugees

by
Matthew Suh, M.D.

Introduction

Although immigration has played a central role in the history of civilization and in the development of nations and continents, the social-psychological dynamics of the process of immigration and resettlement have received relatively limited attention. Traditionally, international migration has been divided into voluntary, or planned, transplantation and involuntary, or forced, migration, comprising refugees, displaced persons, and forced labourers. However, voluntary migration is not always so voluntary. It is at times difficult to determine whether an individual emigrates of his own free will or because of anxiety over anticipated persecution, which may or may not materialize. Psychologically, therefore, a voluntary immigrant may be as much of a refugee as an involuntary immigrant.

Immigration represents an interruption and frustration of natural life expectations, with all the related anxieties and potential damage to the self-concept. Immigration induces intellectual and emotional stress, forcing the immigrant to change his familiar images and build a new mental map. There is much evidence that individuals in severe conflict situations, when facing seemingly insurmountable obstacles, tend to regress to former patterns of behaviour. The individual's integrative capacity is under particular strain when an immigrant starts life in a new country, away from the familiar surroundings that had previously provided some protection or nurture. A mentally healthy person will create conditions to maintain his inner security by satisfying his need for belonging and acquiring the esteem of others. Those who latently or overtly are not in good mental health will be in need of special attention.

Immigration is one of the most obvious instances of complete disorganization of the individual's role system, and some disturbance of social identity and self-image is to be expected. In this sense, immigration has a desocializing effect. The psychological dangers of uprooting, as observed in refugees during and since the Second World War, have been well described by many researchers in the field. It is noted, for instance, that the risk of psychological disorder was especially great when conditions before and after flight were particularly stressful, ranging from sudden disaster to prolonged persecution and danger to life. High rates of transitional emotional reactions were apparent in the initial phases of rescue. These seem to have a self-protective quality in response to stress and bewilderment. Refugees appear to sense this danger intuitively, seeking confrères with whom to cluster in groups. However, the danger to psychological well-being increased when the period between immigration and final settlement was protracted and made difficult by rumours and uncertainties. Another factor influencing adaptation or maladaptation is the possibility or impossibility of returning to the country of origin or migrating to a third country. An immigrant who knows, or believes, he can return to his old environment and maintain close contact abroad may be hesitant to change. Individuals migrating against their will may sabotage themselves unconsciously, refusing to succeed in a country of asylum they did not choose. For instance, many persons who left Hitler's Germany to go to Palestine before the Second World War began a serious study of Hebrew only after Israel obtained independence and they came to realize that they could not or did not want to leave the country.

Immigration as a Process of Adaptation: The Intrapersonal and Interpersonal

Immigration, voluntary or involuntary, produces, like all catastrophies and crises, different traumatic world images within which people seem to demand the sudden assumption of new and often transitory identities: what has motivated and removed the immigrant; how he had been excluded or had excluded himself from his previous home; how he had been transported or had chosen to travel the distance between home and destination; and how he had been kept or had kept himself separate, had been absorbed or had involved himself in his new setting. These situational factors, however, do not account entirely for those inner psychological mechanisms that permit man to maintain and regain in this world of contending forces an individual sense of centrality, of wholeness, and of initiative, which is defined as identity. An approach to these issues begins with the individual and extends to his existence and functioning as part of the social-cultural system.

The individual or intrapsychic viewpoint is epitomized in the concept of ego defence, or psychological mechanisms of defence. Defence mechanisms are activated by anxiety, itself a consequence of unresolved conflict between wishes pressing for conscious expression on one hand and the forces inhibiting such expression on the other. These mechanisms operate automatically and unconsciously to ward off the awareness of breakthrough into consciousness of unaccepted impulses and to reduce anxiety, guilt, or other psychological tension. They keep the tension at a manageable level.

The interplay between individual defensive and adaptive processes is a function of past history and present environmental circumstances. A person's repertoire of defensive and adaptive devices stems from his early experiences, and their use is reinforced or extinguished by current social sanctions and prohibitions. When major changes occur via immigration from one social culture to another, behavioural patterns useful in the old setting may prove maladaptive in the new. Acute sensitivity that permits empathic understanding in one group may be perceived as discomfort-provoking vigilance or heightened level of suspiciousness in another. For example, a particular ethnic group such as the Khmer tend to share inner feelings only with a person's own adult family members; anyone outside a person's individual kinship network wanting to know how he feels about life or his job may succeed only in heightening a sense of suspicion or vigilance. The culturally supported tendency to attribute sources of danger to external factors, reinforced by magical belief systems in rural areas, may interfere seriously with the inward-looking or learning about oneself sometimes necessary for survival in the city. A persisting tendency to blame other persons, groups, or forces for lack of success impairs both motivation and the acquisition of new, more useful responses. Under these circumstances, adaptive failure may occur without a person being aware of it. One index of such failure in the immigrant may be incompatibility between his self-image and a status (of which he is often unaware) given him by the social system.

Immigration as a Process of Social Change

Immigration, a change or shift in residence, involves not only new places, but new faces, new norms, new languages, new environments. Such movement implies the crossing of social system boundaries, whether the systems are defined in terms of national entities, regional subcultures, or immediate friendship and kinship networks. The immigrant leaves behind him the supports and the stresses of the native system from which he departs. He loses the support of social and geographic familiarity, of long-term relationships and values that were built into him while growing up. At the same time, he is freed of some of the stress of disease and hunger, of the obligation to perform in expected ways, and of certain stressful relationships. He is welcomed by the host system or must deal with resistances in the new system to which he comes. He is excited by new stimuli and opportunities and fearful of new threats and the unknown. Between the two systems, en route, he must cope with a series of transitional factors that colour his perceptions, attitudes, and capacity to deal with the host environment. His adaptation throughout is shaped by internal motives for moving, which may have little to do with environmental push or pull factors. Some of these motives are best described as idiosyncratic-psychological. They are the distillates of ungratified wishes and needs, undischarged tensions, and unresolved conflicts. Voluntary migrants anticipate their moves, and as decisions are made and preparations begun, they are caught up in the process of change. The ability to change, therefore, is of utmost importance in the immigrant's ability to adapt in the new host system. Change and adaptation, however, are not automatic. They are determined by talent, social contacts, and the degree to which the immediate consequences of moving fit the pre-immigratory ideas and fantasies. The initial encounters in the new environment may be especially potent in this regard.

Immigration and Mental Illness

Although it is generally being maintained in the literature and by the public that the immigrant population tends to show higher admission rates to mental hospitals, more recent carefully conducted studies seem to dispute such epidemiological data. The exception to this general observation is the detection of much more psychiatric illness in immigrants from a rural, lower socio-economic origin than among immigrants from an urban, middle-class socio-economic origin and the native-born. When it comes to the refugees, however, there is very little disagreement that the rates of psychiatric illness among refugees is rather high.

Over the course of the years, there has been a refinement in research and statistical procedures concerning immigrants and refugees, and now it is generally observed that special attention must be paid to the following three factors in conducting any meaningful studies of the mental health problems of the immigrants and refugees: (1) the characteristics of the immigrant, namely, his pre-immigration and post-immigration personality and adaptational pattern; (2) the motivation behind his immigration; and (3), the type of environment in which the immigrant settles.

Implications for Resettlement and Readjustment

In considering current programs of assistance to refugees, the most important characteristic seems to be that they are planned. This means that every effort is made to meet as adequately as possible the individual needs of the refugee and expectations of the receiving community. Families should be kept together as a unit; children should not be separated from parents. The long-range goal is effective adaptation and integration into the host country.

If involuntary immigration is perceived as a process of desocialization, then adaptation in the host country may be seen as a process of resocialization. In this regard, much emphasis must be placed in the absorptive capacity of the receiving community and its socio-economic and psychological readiness to accept immigrants. The community must be prepared to allow the immigrant time to learn before he can be expected to assume a role and social identity meaningful in terms of the new society. Receiving communities should provide a warm reception and immediate access to social networks, combatting the isolation and the loneliness that engender psychological disturbances and psychosomatic disorders. Suitable means of communication should be fostered, including newsletters in the immigrant's native language. Desocialization tendencies are slowly eliminated while resocialization forces expand. An effort is made to re-establish the role set, to rebuild the connections between self-image and the role image, and to achieve a real and acceptable social status. Adaptation is not a well-ordered transitory sequence of phases of adjustment, but a fluid exchange between the immigrant and society. There is general consensus that immigrants well briefed on their new social-cultural environment tend to adapt more rapidly than those who are ill informed. Similarly, those for whom life is better than, or in accord with, the pre-immigratory expectations tend to feel much more at home in their new community and constitute less of a psychosocial risk. Immigrants must be given time to reflect on the novelty of new experiences and to regain the inner security and self-respect so essential to effective continuation of normal life processes.

The Boat People in Canada

There is a basic difference, as noted before, between an immigrant and a refugee. The first has a free choice, which implies the immigrant has many possibilities of motivation; the refugee has no choice. He has no place to go back to. The "boat people" and other Indochinese refugees in Canada face an extremely difficult situation of resettlement and adaptation for the following reasons:

1. They were forced to leave their country of origin; that is, they felt they had no choice and no say in leaving their homeland, had no choice in coming to Canada as opposed to other countries. They constitute essentially a group of unwilling immigrants.

2. Some were an ethnic minority in their own country, and being forced to leave, they see themselves being condemned to live as refugees, totally unprepared and unequipped, in an alien cultural environment.

3. Being refugees, very little kinship support exists, as opposed to voluntary immigrants who may have relatives and sponsors already here; thus their survival, at least in their own eyes, is a very precarious undertaking.

4. Racial and linguistic differences would prove to be a major barrier to rapid adaptation to and integration into the host culture.

5. Since many are of rural background, forced urbanization would further impede these refugees' resettlement, adaptation, and mental well-being.

Clinical Problems of the Immigrant and Refugee

If the immigrant has strong motivation initially to leave his native land in search of a better opportunity abroad, he will prepare himself psychologically for the process of loss, grief, mourning, re-establishment of new attachment behaviour and come to terms with the newly found psychologically satisfying interpersonal relationship, which may in an ideal case completely replace the old satisfying relationship he left behind. Even in such an ideal case, the process of successful grief and mourning is not without its own risks. In the case of an immigrant who comes here as a refugee, the process of successful mourning is extremely arduous and fraught with psychological dangers.

The process of adjustment of refugees to a new culture is commonly and popularly referred to as "culture shock." It may be easier to understand the phenomenon of culture shock if it is viewed on a continuum. At one end in its most extreme form is the situation of the refugee from a totally different sociocultural and racial background facing a new and alien culture as a result of a move not of his own choosing. At the other extreme the situation is less stressful and adaptation a less formidable task when the immigrant's cultural expectations and orientations are compatible with those in the host country. It is shown, for instance, that the English-speaking immigrants from the United Kingdom coming to Canada or the United States, or the Chinese going to Singapore, integrate and assimilate with much more ease than other ethnic groups. In its least drastic form, it may be likened to the situation of a person needing some time to unwind when he first goes on vacation. He has yet to assume the role of a vacationer or a tourist, and thus some form of stress, albeit very mild, may occur if he happens to be highly work-oriented.

The person who undergoes a drastic cultural change rather suddenly with little or no preparation or motivation may experience a wider variety of emotions. As would be expected, he will have to cope with the sense of anxiety about dealing with unfamiliar cultural norms and demands where he does not know the social cues of behaviour, nor the language, and has no means of support.

Depression

Depression is the most commonly felt and experienced state, and it may reach the proportions of becoming a grief reaction if it is not dealt with appropriately. It is reasonable, therefore, to recognize that people who leave their home culture, and whose move is not of their own choosing, will go through the same cluster of symptoms as one would see in the case of bereavement. The depression, anxiety, and feelings of isolation and loneliness may manifest themselves in various ways. There may be changes in sleep patterns, appetite, activity level, energy level, and so forth. The person may become irritable, may at times seem not to be co-operative and at times very suspicious and sensitive. As with any grieving process, the management includes understanding, time, and an outlet for expressing fears, apprehensions, and frustrations. If the person can be helped to verbalize his or her experiences and to accept the loss and deal with it in the usual human way, it will eventually pass.

It is reasonable, therefore, to expect that in most people there will be either an obvious or less obvious mourning process as the old culture and familiar ties are replaced, at least in part, by the new ones. Since these are normal and expected feelings, one may ask how one goes about deciding when the process has become abnormal or pathological. In general, if a person is able to continue to deal relatively effectively with his environment and social demands and with the tasks presented to him in spite of the feelings that he is experiencing, one may assume that the feelings are probably not abnormal or pathological. It is when the feelings become presistent over time, do not change, and begin to interfere with effective adaptation that he may find himself in need of professional help. For example, the feeling of sadness would be expected, it would come and go, and the person would be expected to feel a sense of nostalgia, of longing, a sense of yearning for the home country that would be rather intense early on and then gradually abate if he succeeds in finding a replacement of what he lost or left behind. If that feeling of sadness became so persis-tent, pervasive, and intense that the person, over a two- or three-week period, was seen crying most of the time, did not eat, was not interested in his new surroundings or other people, was not sleeping properly, seemed very tired, was not taking care of his grooming or personal hygiene, then one could conclude that a mental disturbance such as a depression, a depressive illness, was present.

Anxiety

The psychological problems of difficulty in adaptation may manifest themselves as anxiety. One would certainly expect that given the language barrier — the lack of social cues — that anxiety would be a common feeling. Apprehensiveness, perhaps even fear, which would be manifested by sweaty palms, shakiness, dry mouth, even headaches, nausea, vomiting, light-headedness, again on a periodic basis, would not be uncommon. When these feelings become prominent, present all the time, interfered with effective adaptation or discharge of social and occupational demands, or with family life, then some professional help would be necessary. There is certainly no clear-cut distinction and one can readily see that the normal and abnormal blend readily and imperceptibly. If a fairly good and trusting relationship exists between the helper and the refugee, then letting the refugee express his fears, frustrations, hopes, and aspirations for a better life is very useful and therapeutic. In the case of an uncommunicative and withdrawn refugee whose cultural norms, attitudes, and beliefs make it difficult to talk freely about his inner feelings, it is often useful to have the services of an intermediary person who speaks the language and can mediate between the two conflicting cultures.

In general, therefore, the management of the psychological aspects of the refugee will not require basically a very professionalized help when he, in spite of depressive feelings, seems to be adapting in an effective way with the new country and the new environment. Since we are dealing here with the fact of loss, fear of being abandoned, grieving over the lost country, and so forth, realistically, there is nothing one can do about it except to offer sympathetic ears. It is often seen that people who are in a position of being helpers tend to feel that they should do more than just listen, that they should be able to do something in a tangible way to take away the sad feelings, the frustrations and make the newcomer happy, make the person feel better. These things are impossible. It is more therapeutic to help those in acute grief successfully mourn the multiple losses and find new psychological objects of attachment, be it a job, a new way of life, or a new mate.

Major Psychiatric Illness

In all cases of moderate depression and anxiety, however, one cannot entirely ignore the possibility of physical harm or death to the individual or to someone else. The possibility of a person committing suicide is a very real one, and a refugee certainly runs a higher risk, at least in the initial stage of adjustment. Some of the more common clues for detecting potential suicides include the presence of a persistent feeling of depression and sadness, of loss, associated with disturbances in sleep, appetite, sexual functions, loss of interest in things one used to enjoy before, and indifference leading to apathy. The person may feel and act very much alone. One of the common ways of finding out if a person is contemplating suicide is to talk to him about the issue. One does not necessarily have to ask a question bluntly, but certainly in the course of conversation it is permissible to ask whether the person feels that life is no longer worth living or that family and friends would be better off without him around. Experience has shown that, asked skillfully but to the point, the potential suicide usually confirms his deep sense of hopelessness and helplessness. When the answers to these questions are in the affirmative, professional help should be sought quickly, perhaps through the emergency department of a local hospital or with the available consultant psychiatrist, if there is one.

More severe disturbances are not infrequent either. These may take an overt and visible form of psychosis, either as the end result of accumulated psychological disturbances manifesting themselves in the form of schizophrenia or paranoid psychosis, or as a result of something physical and organic, such as an elderly person experiencing both the impact of aging and the psychological problems of growing old in an alien country. However, some major forms of psychoses should only be handled by well-trained mental health professionals and, in particular, psychiatrists and the general practitioners. It is not difficult to know when a person is psychotic: he has lost touch with reality, behaving in a bizarre or uninhibitedly impulsive manner, with extreme fluctuations of mood, and with pronounced disturbances in thought processes, such as delusions of persecution or grandeur, or abnormal experiences in perception, such as hallucinations. No well-meant counselling will do in these cases of major psychoses, and the patient should be immediately referred to a general practitioner or directly to a psychiatrist.

Conclusion

It is apparent that, with the exception of the actual major mental illnesses, most of the adjustment problems that create difficulties and stresses in the individual and his or her family can be handled with a timely and sympathetic approach by helpers and sponsors. Time also is a greater helper in this regard. It can be stated very firmly that adjustmental problems are inversely related to the failure or success in acculturation and assimilation into the host country's main stream of life.

Conclusion

Cambodian children at a camp in Thailand.

Towards the Future

by
David Wurfel

This volume was inspired by the tragedy of the refugee exodus from Kampuchea, Laos, and Vietnam and by the need to understand better those whom we have decided to welcome to Canada. We have tried to explain why the refugees left their homelands and why resettlement outside Southeast Asia is the only hope for a secure future for most of them.

Perhaps we have not emphasized enough what a severe psychological trauma this process of uprooting is. The decision to leave the land of one's birth, to abandon family, friends, and the culture that has given meaning to one's life — not to mention one's property — is very difficult indeed. A number of refugees in Canada have even contemplated returning home, especially after the first winter.

It should be clear that most refugees, under different conditions, would never have left Indochina. And, in fact, most Vietnamese, Hoa, Lao, and Khmer, under identical conditions, have stayed, even though many may have considered leaving. Most refugees who are now in camps cannot remain in Southeast Asia, so that welcoming them to Canada is both necessary and proper. And while they are in camps, we have a moral obligation to help make life bearable. The CUSO (Canadian University Services Overseas) project in Thailand is a wise use of Canadian resources to this end.

If we have a general concern for the welfare of the peoples of Indochina — and not just for those we are able to bring under our wings in Canada — we must now look beyond the servicing of refugees here and examine what we might do to help reduce the pressures that create refugees there. Surely that is the way we can assist the most people, with the least cost to ourselves, to do what they would prefer to do anyway — prosper in their own land. A constructive Canadian foreign policy toward Southeast Asia would put top priority on helping the people there to help themselves.

The refugee flow has been caused basically by the denial of human rights (or the fear of that prospect), by economic hardship, and by international conflict. What can Canada do to help alter these conditions?

The denial of human rights may stem from ancient prejudices, such as those against the Chinese in Indochina. These attitudes are well beyond the boundaries of any potential Canadian influence and must be accepted as given within the complex skein of problems we want to help solve. We have already noted how ethnic tensions are activated by political or economic crisis, however, so that the overt manifestation of prejudice may be contained indirectly.

Human rights violations are also a common historical adjunct of revolutionary change — though in the Third World today they are even more frequently associated with counter-revolutionary repression. It cannot, of course, be Canadian policy to interfere directly in the political system of another sovereign state. But we can provide inducements that will lessen the hardships.

Economic difficulties always contribute to the unpopularity of a regime, and often to that regime's super-sensitivity to criticism. Economic progress, on the other hand, makes a regime both more popular and more tolerant. Well-designed economic aid in Indochina could thus contribute to a diminution of the refugee flow in two ways: (1) by reducing the economic incentive for those contemplating flight; and (2) by increasing the tolerance of difference by both regime and population. In my opinion, an immediate resumption of Canadian economic aid to Vietnam and a modest expansion of the large trickle now going to Kampuchea are certainly in order. And Laos deserves the same treatment.

The "punishment" of Vietnam for human rights violations in 1979 by cutting off all Canadian aid merely increased economic hardship, encouraged more refugees to leave, and decreased the possibility of a softening on human rights, not to mention driving the Vietnamese more securely into the arms of the Russians — an inopportune move indeed! The communication with another government, which the transfer of economic aid requires, provides an opportunity for some leverage on human rights questions. Canada might quite appropriately indicate, however, that further expansion of economic aid would be linked, in part, to the human

Condominas, George. "L'entraide agricole chez les Mnong Gar (Proto-Indochinois du Vietnam central)," *Études Rurales*, nos. 53–56 (1974), pp. 407-20.

Delvert, Jean. *Le paysan Cambodgien*. Paris: Mouton & Co., 1963.

Études Rurales. *Agriculture et sociétés en Asie du Sud-Est*. Special, nos. 53–56. Paris: Mouton & Co., 1974.

Fischer, C.A. *South-east Asia: A Social, Economic and Political Geography*. 2d ed. London: Methuen, 1966.

Gourou, Pierre. *L'Utilisation du sol en Indochine française*. Paris: Paul Hartman, 1940.

Gourou, Pierre. *Les paysans du Delta Tonkinois*, 1936. Reprint. Paris: Mouton & Co., 1965.

Hanks, Lucien M. *Rice and Man: Agricultural Ecology in Southeast Asia*. Chicago: Aldine-Atherton, 1972.

LeBar, Frank M.; Hickey, Gerald C.; and Musgrave, John K. *Ethnic Groups of Mainland Southeast Asia*. New Haven: Human Relations Area Files Press, 1964.

MacKinnon, J. and K. *Les animaux d'Asie: Ecologie de la région indo-malaisie*. Paris: Nathan, 1976.

Mus, Paul. *L'angle de l'Asie*. Paris: Hartman, 1977.

Spencer, J.E. *Shifting Cultivation in Southeastern Asia*. Berkeley: University of California Press, 1966.

Spencer, J.E. "La maîtrise de l'eau en Asie du Sud-Est," *Études Rurales*, nos. 53–56 (1974), pp. 73–94.

Chapter 6

General Southeast Asia

Alexander, Garth. *Silent Invasion: The Chinese in Southeast Asia* (1973).
An account by a British journalist who believes that the Chinese, inadvertently, have had a major political role in Southeast Asia; sympathetic to the Chinese plight.

Burling, Robbins. *Hill Farms and Padi Fields: Life in Mainland Southeast Asia*. Englewood Cliffs, N.J.: Prentice-Hall, 1965.

Bibliography

General

Southeast Asian Refugees, newsletter published by Employment and Immigration Canada, Public Affairs Division, Ottawa.

Chapter 4

The Boat People: An "Age" Investigation with Bruce Grant. London: Penguin Books, 1979.
An excellent, up-to-the minute account of the whole problem.

Those Who Leave (the "problem of Vietnamese refugees"). Hanoi: Vietnam Courier, 1979.
The Vietnamese side of the story. Should be available from the Vietnamese embassy in Ottawa.

Tsai Maw-Kuey. *Les Chinois au Sud-Vietnam.* Paris: Bibliothèque Nationale (Ministère de l'Education National, Comité des travaux historiques et scientifiques, Memoires de la section de géographie, no. 3), 1968.
Dated and biased, but the only book available on the subject.

Willmott, W.E. *The Chinese in Cambodia.* Vancouver: University of British Columbia Press, 1967.
Dated and biased, but one of only two books on the subject, both by the same author.

Willmott, W.E. "The Chinese in Southeast Asia," *Australian Outlook* 20 (1966):252-62.

Woodside, Alexander B. "Nationalism and Party in the Breakdown of Sino-Vietnamese Relations," *Pacific Affairs* 52 (1979):381-409.

Chapter 5

Barrau, Jacques. "L'Asie du Sud-Est, berceau cultural," *Études Rurales*, nos. 53-56 (1974), pp. 17-40.

Brocheux, Pierre, and Hemery, Daniel. "Le Vietnam exsangue," *Le Monde Diplomatique*, no. 312 (1980), pp. 15-18.

rights situation in the recipient country. At the same time, we might make a special offer for the acceptance of political prisoners (occupants of "re-education camps") into Canada, taking care not to admit those with criminal records.

Foreign economic assistance has another, very different, but equally powerful rationale in Indochina. We have noted that intensification of the Sino-Soviet dispute sharpened Sino-Vietnamese and Vietnamese-Kampuchean conflict. Only when Vietnam and Kampuchea can diversify their international contacts, reducing the present dependence on the USSR, can conflict be defused. The variety of countries now trying to save Kampuchea from starvation is thus encouraging on political as well as on humanitarian grounds. Canadian generosity there should expand.

With such generosity, Canada would then have a stronger voice in trying to arrange the terms for withdrawal of Vietnamese troops from Kampuchea. This should not be simply a reflection of Peking's position, but an independent Canadian stance designed to produce the concessions from Thailand — such as halting Chinese aid through Thai territory to the Pol Pot remnants — which will surely be necessary to get Vietnamese forces to pull back. A more representative government in Phnom Penh needs also to be negotiated, and then recognized. Canada's earlier role in the International Control Commission gives her greater diplomatic background than most other "middle powers" on this question.

The United States, which has a profound obligation to contribute to the economic rehabilitation of Indochina, does not now seem to be in a mood to fulfil it. Therefore, it is even more important for other Western states to make such a contribution, within the limits of capability, both for immediate humanitarian reasons and to reduce the prospects of future refugee-generating conflict there.

If our compassion is genuine, we will try to understand the origins of the Southeast Asian refugees in Canada in order to facilitate their resettlement better. But, at the same time, we will make a more active contribution to economic rehabilitation and the peaceful settlement of that region's political disputes so that the human desperation that leads to flight from homelands will no longer be necessary.

Canada remains one of the most richly endowed countries in the world, both in human and natural resources. This contribution to peace and economic well-being in Indochina we *can* make if we have the foresight and the will to do so.

An authoritative critique of the origins of the National Liberation Front and the subsequent American role.

Luce, Don, and Sommer, John. *Viet Nam: The Unheard Voices.* Ithaca: Cornell University Press, 1969.
The best work on South Vietnam in the 1960s, by Americans in the International Voluntary Service; organized topically.

McAlister, John T., Jr., and Mus, Paul. *The Vietnamese and Their Revolution.* New York, Evanston, and London: Harper & Row, 1970.
Translated essays of a leading French scholar on Vietnam.

Nhat-Hanh, Thich. *Vietnam: Lotus in a Sea of Fire.* New York: Hill and Wang, 1967.
A Buddhist view and a description of the Buddhist role.

Taylor, Charles. *Snow Job: Canada, the United States and Vietnam.* Toronto: Anansi, 1974.
A detailed critique of the Canadian role up to 1973.

Terzani, T. *Giai Phong! The Fall and Liberation of Saigon* (1976).
A fascinating account by an Italian journalist who remained in Saigon throughout; sympathetic to, but not uncritical of, the liberation forces.

Woodside, Alexander B. *Community and Revolution in Modern Vietnam.* Boston: Houghton, 1976.
The only major historical survey by a Canadian scholar, and perhaps the best.

Kampuchea

Grant, J.S., ed. *Cambodia: The Widening War in Indochina.* New York: Washington Square Press, 1971.

Osborne, Milton. *Politics and Power in Cambodia: The Sihanouk Years.* Camberwell, Victoria: Longmans Australia, 1973.
Australian specialist on Cambodia covers the twentieth century to 1970.

Steinberg, David Joel, ed. *Cambodia: Its People, Its Society, Its Culture.* New Haven: Human Relations Area Files Press, 1957.

Willmott, William E. *The Chinese in Cambodia.* Vancouver: University of British Columbia Press, 1967.

The most comprehensive — yet compact — study in any language; by a leading Canadian scholar.

Willmott, William E. *The Political Structure of the Chinese Community in Cambodia*. London: Athlone Press, 1970. More narrowly focused than the previous study.

Laos

Adams, Nina S., and McCoy, Alfred W., eds. *Laos: War and Revolution*. New York: Harper & Row, 1970.

Berval, Rene de. *Kingdom of Laos*. Saigon: France-Asie, 1959. A survey of virtually all aspects of Lao life and culture with many articles by Lao authors. Translated from the French.

LeBar, Frank M., and Suddard, Adrienne, eds. *Laos: Its People, Its Society, Its Culture*. New Haven: Human Relations Area Files Press, 1960.

Chapter 10

Brodrick, Alan H. *Little Vehicle: Cambodia and Laos.* London and New York: Hutchinson, 1949.

Burling, Robbins. *Hill Farms and Padi Fields: Life in Mainland Southeast Asia*. Englewood Cliffs, N.J.: Prentice-Hall, 1965.

Keesing, Roger M. *Cultural Anthropology*. New York: Holt, Rinehart and Winston, 1976.

Keyes, Charles F. *The Golden Peninsula: Culture and Adaptation in Mainland Southeast Asia*. New York: Macmillan, 1977.

Lester, Robert C. *Theravada Buddhism in Southeast Asia*. Ann Arbor: University of Michigan Press, 1973.

Liu, William T. *Transition to Nowhere*. Nashville: Charter House Publishers, 1979.

Porée-Maspero, Eveline. *Étude sur les rites agraires des Cambodgiens*. 3 vols. Paris: Mouton & Co., 1962–69.

Scott, James C. *The Moral Economy of the Peasant: Rebellion and Subsistence in Southeast Asia*. New Haven and London: Yale University Press, 1976.

The Boat People: An "Age" Investigation with Bruce Grant. London: Penguin Books, 1979.